Spiders CLOWNS, and GREAT MOLE RATS

Over 150 Phobias That Will FREAK YOU OUT, from ARACHNOPHOBIA to ZEMMIPHOBIA

ANDREW THOMPSON

ULYSSES PRESS

Published in the U.S. by:
ULYSSES PRESS
P.O. Box 3440
Berkeley, CA 94703
www.ulyssespress.com

ISBN: 978-1-61243-932-7
Library of Congress Control Number: 2019905479

10 9 8 7 6 5 4 3 2 1

Printed in Canada by Marquis Book Printing

Acquisitions Editor: Bridget Thoreson
Managing Editor: Claire Chun
Project Editor: Claire Sielaff
Editor: Jessica Benner
Proofreaders: Lauren Harrison and Renee Rutledge
Cover and interior design: Jake Flaherty
Cover artwork: background © Lukasz Szwaj/shutterstock.com; spider web © Alexey Grigorev/shutterstock.com; clown © Rusty Letter Images; mole rat © Morphart Creation/shutterstock.com
Interior artwork: see page 269

Contents

L Is For Linonophobia 140

M Is For Melophobia 152

N Is For Nephophobia 167

Introduction

Phobia? What Phobia?

pho•bi•a (noun)—an abnormally extreme fear or dislike of a particular thing or situation, especially one that does not have a rational explanation. [Origin: via Latin from Greek *phobos*, meaning "fear."]

Well, that's about it in a nutshell. An irrational fear.

There are literally hundreds of phobias out there, and for those with a particularly jumpy disposition, there's a fear to suit every need and occasion. Everybody's heard of the fear of heights (acrophobia) and, thanks to the 1990 horror film *Arachnophobia*, most of us know about the fear of spiders. But what about the unusual pogonophobia (fear of beards), phasmophobia (fear of ghosts), or gynophobia (fear of women)? Then there's the downright extraordinary omphalophobia (fear of belly buttons), taphophobia (fear of being buried alive), and kinemortophobia (fear of zombies. Yes, *zombies*). How did they all come about?

And why the strange and unpronounceable names? Why not just call it zombiphobia so everyone knows exactly what you're scared of? As Shakespeare said, "It's all Greek to me." The word *phobia* derives from the Greek word *phobos*, so nearly all of the phobia prefixes are Greek. Coulrophobia is the fear of clowns (of which Johnny Depp is a genuine sufferer). The "coul" comes from the Greek *kolon*, meaning "limb" in the sense of "stilt walker" or clown. *Spiders, Clowns, and Great Mole Rats* explains the origins of over 150 phobias and lets you in on a host of trivia for each one, like which celebrities are afflicted.

Did you know that alektorophobia is the fear of chickens? Yes, the small, flightless bird. And that Gustave Eiffel, designer of the Eiffel Tower, was actually an acrophobe? Some xanthophobes (who are afraid of the color yellow) refuse to leave the house on a sunny day, while triskaidekaphobes (who are terrified of the number 13) won't venture outside on the 13th of the month. And did you know that didaskaleinophobia is a fear of school (a trait that Mark Twain's Tom Sawyer didn't technically have, despite his frequent truancy)? Or that hippopotomonstrosesquippedaliophobia, ironically one of the longest words in the English language, is actually a fear of long words? Are you familiar with koumpounophobia, the fear of buttons, a condition that Steve Jobs was afflicted with, leading him to the development of the touchscreen iPhone? It's time to find out all this and more.

Spiders, Clowns, and Great Mole Rats explains the fascinating origins of more than 150 bizarre phobias in an alphabetical journey through nearly every fear known to man, from the weird to the wonderful, the eccentric to the funny and, at times, the downright unbelievable. By the end of this book, you'll know nearly everything there is to be afraid of.

But remember, as Franklin D. Roosevelt (a sufferer of triskaidekaphobia) famously said, "the only thing we have to fear is fear itself." Fortunately, there's a phobia for that as well—phobophobia. Good luck out there!

Is for
Alektorophobia

Ablutophobia

MEANING: fear of washing

ORIGIN: the Latin word *ablut- ere*, meaning "to wash off"

ABLUTOPHOBIA is the unwarranted fear of washing, bathing, or cleaning. This rare phobia is most prevalent in women and children, especially those with an emotional disposition. Ablutophobia is thought to be a legacy from the 16th century, when bathing was not a commonplace practice in Europe. Back then, too much washing was considered unhealthy, and most Europeans displayed symptoms of ablutophobia. While today bathing is very much encouraged (and almost essential if you're going to socialize), some European descendants still suffer from the condition. Traumatic causes, like a bad experience slipping in the bath and hurting yourself, can cause ablutophobia, as can watching really scary bath-related movie scenes, like the troubling shower scene in *Psycho*. The idea of bathing induces breathlessness, nausea, and clouded thinking, resulting in an inability to bathe, shower, clean the house, or wash clothes. In severe cases, victims end up living in extremely unsanitary environments and, as a result, become prone to illness and disease. Neuro-linguistic programming, as well as hypnosis, have been used to treat this debilitating phobia. Sometimes medication is used, as recovery is essential if the sufferer is going to have any form of social life, because, let's face it, nobody likes hanging around someone who stinks. That said, just because you do a dirty job for a living doesn't mean you have ablutopho-bia—that is, unless you don't bathe regularly.

THINGS TO AVOID: baths; showers; taps; swimming pools; oceans and other bodies of water; water generally; the song *Ablutophobia* by New Zealand artist Sheep, Dog & Wolf; the 2006 comedic play *The Mistakes Madeline Made*, which features a character who develops ablutophobia; the *Friends* episode "The One with Joey's Dirty Day"; the Bobby Darin song "Splish Splash."

|||| Phobia Trivia ||||

Elizabeth I of England, who reigned as queen from 1558 to 1603, famously said, "I take a bath once a month whether I need it or not." But far from being an ablutophobe, she was actually known as one of the cleanest people in Europe. Despite displaying symptoms of the condition, the populace weren't ablutophobes (well, some of them probably were); bathing facilities were just simply not commonplace.

|||| Statistics ||||

According to a 2014 study, 66 percent of Americans shower at least once a day, while 24 percent admit to not washing their hands all the time after using a public toilet.

Achondroplasiaphobia

MEANING: fear of little people

ORIGIN: the medical term *achondroplasia*, which is a skeletal disorder of the cartilage that forms during the fetal stage and leads to dwarfism

Also known as nanosophobia and the oddly named lollypop-guildophobia, ACHONDROPLASIAPHOBIA is the undue fear of dwarves. This phobia usually arises because of a traumatic childhood experience with a little person, such as a school janitor or daycare worker behaving badly. As little people often appear abnormal, with disproportionately large heads, there is also an evolutionary basis for the fear: People are inherently uncomfortable with anyone who looks different. Achondroplasiaphobia can also arise from the misguided belief that little people have alien origins or possess magical or spiritual powers (like leprechauns). Films and books also have historically cast little people in a negative light, which can also lead to the condition (even in *Snow White*, the dwarves, while friendly, lived in the forest, suggesting they'd been cast out of society). Whatever the cause, achondroplasiaphobia can be a debilitating illness, with sufferers often having nightmares, sometimes waking up screaming, as well as feeling the overwhelming urge to flee if presented with the object of their terror. In extreme cases, the mere image or mention of a little person can set off a full-blown panic attack, with symptoms like rapid breathing, dry mouth, shaking, and hysterical crying. Achondroplasiaphobia can indeed affect a person's ability to function normally on a day-to-day basis, with most sufferers refusing to go to circuses, casinos, malls, or fairs where little people are likely to be present. The most successful method of treatment is educating the achondroplasiaphobe so that they can overcome stereotypical notions and to realize that little people merely have a congenital disorder and are not evil or harmful. Medication is also sometimes used, as is desensitization therapy, which involves the gradual introduction of little people into the sufferer's life until their presence is no longer a source of abject fear and dread.

THINGS TO AVOID: circuses; casinos; fairs; malls; *Snow White and the Seven Dwarfs* (books and films); *Charlie and the Chocolate Factory* (books and films); *Game of Thrones*; dwarf-throwing contests.

For reasons unknown, actress Lindsay Lohan is believed to suffer from achondroplasiaphobia.

Dwarfism in humans is defined as an adult height of less than 4 feet 10 inches, regardless of sex, and occurs in 4 to 15 out of every 100,000 people.

Ailurophobia

MEANING: fear of cats

ORIGIN: the Greek word *ailouros*, meaning "cat"

Also known as elurophobia, aelurophobia, felinophobia, and gatophobia, AILUROPHOBIA is the irrational fear of cats. Cats are predatory by nature, often hissing and scratching, and this is thought to be the primary cause of the phobia. Their association with witchcraft, folklore, and evil is also a possible cause, as is a child seeing other people, such as a parent or even a cartoon character, behave fearfully toward cats. The fact that cats were revered in some cultures, most notably ancient Egypt, can also lead to ailurophobia, because of the belief by some that cats were superior to humans. People who suffer from this phobia can suffer panic attacks upon an encounter with a cat, fleeing the scene or fighting in defense, and will do anything to avoid a cat, even if it entails putting themselves at risk, such as running across a busy street. Ailurophobes also avoid the homes of friends who have pet cats, and will even sometimes carry cat food snacks around to throw as a diversionary tactic. While some people only fear big cats, like lions and tigers, others fear the smaller cats as well, afraid of being bitten, scratched, stared at with scary yellow eyes, or surprised by an encounter in the dark, especially with a black cat that will bring bad luck (as the superstition goes). But it is not all bad news for the ailurophobe, as the condition is usually treatable with exposure therapy. This involves first touching velvet fabrics before acclimatizing to a feline in toy form, then, eventually, as the symptoms of extreme panic decrease, being introduced to a fluffy live kitten.

THINGS TO AVOID: cats of all sizes and breeds; Africa; the *Cats* musical and soundtrack; *The Lion King*; the comic strip *Big Nate*, the title character of which has ailurophobia; the 1969 horror film *Eye of the Cat*, where the main character planning the murder of an old woman has the phobia; many nature documentaries.

||||| Phobia Trivia |||||

Ailurophobia has affected many famous personalities throughout history, including Julius Caesar, Alexander the Great, Napoleon Bonaparte, Genghis Khan, Benito Mussolini, William Shakespeare, Adolf Hitler, and Louis XIV. In more modern times, other notable sufferers of this condition are American

Impractical Joker Sal Vulcano, and Xiumin, a member of the South Korean–Chinese boy band Exo, who developed the condition after being attacked by a cat as a child. Cats are able to see in the dark because they have a great number of rod photoreceptor cells, which are responsible for peripheral and night vision. They do, however, lack many cone receptors used for day vision and color perception, making them sensitive to excess light, which is why their slit-like pupils close narrowly in bright conditions. So, what does this mean for the ailurophobe? If you come face to face with a hostile cat, you'd better hope that you're in a blindingly bright room and wearing a colorful shirt.

||||| Statistics |||||

This is quite a common phobia, with an estimated 22 percent of Americans afflicted to some degree. The International Cat Association currently recognizes 71 standardized breeds of cats.

Alektorophobia

MEANING: fear of chickens

ORIGIN: the Greek word *alektor*, meaning "rooster"

ALEKTOROPHOBIA is an extreme fear of chickens and is predominantly related to the live birds and the perceived danger of attack. It is a surprisingly rare phobia, and in some cases can also relate to the meat and eggs of the bird. It is also not just seeing chickens in person that can cause panic; images or photographs are often enough to trigger a negative reaction.

Most alektorophobes are not born with the condition but can trace it to a specific traumatic experience at a young age. Manifesting with symptoms such as nausea, dry mouth, shaking, and an inability to speak, the phobia tends to worsen as a person ages. Given that chickens are a fairly common animal, living with a fear of them can be very difficult to manage, especially for rural folk. Alektorophobia is treated by medication, hypnotherapy, or energy techniques like tai chi, meditation, and positive visualization. The leading treatment, however, is exposure therapy, where chickens are gradually introduced into the patient's life, starting with pictures or videos before the small flightless birds are presented in the flesh.

THINGS TO AVOID: Foghorn Leghorn cartoons and merchandise; cockfights (see Phobia Trivia below); counting your chickens before they hatch; KFC; the "why did the chicken cross the road?" joke, particularly if you also suffer from agyrophobia (fear of crossing the street).

||||| Phobia Trivia |||||

Contrary to popular belief (at least among alektorophobes), chickens are not actually all that dangerous. In fact, there is only one known case of a person being killed by a chicken (actually a rooster). The victim was a spectator at a cockfight in Tulare County, California, in 2011, and the culprit fowl had a knife strapped to its leg to enhance its fighting power, which it used to stab the man. That said, dead chickens are far more dangerous. Foodborne illnesses are commonly contracted from eating chickens and their eggs.

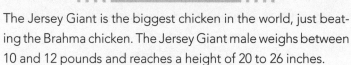

The Jersey Giant is the biggest chicken in the world, just beating the Brahma chicken. The Jersey Giant male weighs between 10 and 12 pounds and reaches a height of 20 to 26 inches.

Allodoxaphobia

MEANING: fear of opinions

ORIGIN: the Greek words *allo*, meaning "different," and *dox*, meaning "opinion"

An extremely rare phobia, ALLODOXAPHOBIA is the fear of opinions, specifically hearing other people's opinions. Sufferers refuse to participate in any activity that may involve being judged by others, and will also avoid answering questions and engaging in conversations, often to the detriment of their personal and professional lives. The allodoxaphobe usually avoids any confrontation or argument that could lead to another's opinion, as that may lead to nausea, shallow breathing, and aggressive displays of anger. Parents and teachers are thought to be the primary cause of allodoxaphobia developing in children, as constant rebukes or criticism can trigger the condition. Inability to properly express an opinion, or having one's opinions regularly rejected, can also lead to allodoxaphobia. Unfortunately, treatment for allodoxaphobia tends to be arduous, drawn out, and largely futile, as it usually involves input from a therapist that the sufferer may perceive as opinion—exactly what the allodoxaphobe is afraid of in the first place.

THINGS TO AVOID: politicians; talk shows; newspapers and nearly all forms of media; most social gatherings and people in general.

While allodoxaphobia is the fear of hearing other people's opinions, the related doxaphobia is the fear of expressing one's own opinions.

While the number of sufferers is unknown, allodoxaphobia is a rare condition and is often found in lists of the weirdest and most unusual phobias.

Amnesiphobia

MEANING: fear of amnesia

ORIGIN: the Greek words *a*, meaning "no," and *mnes*, meaning "memory"

Also known as amnesiophobia, AMNESIPHOBIA is the fear of amnesia, that is, the loss of memory or inability to recall past experiences. This condition usually develops when a person experiences memory loss, such as forgetting a significant event. This episodic amnesia makes the person fearful of experiencing the same issue again. Witnessing friends or family members suffer from amnesia can also lead to the phobia. Sufferers generally experience uncontrollable anxiety, feeling a loss of control, and an overwhelming desire to flee even when there is nothing specific to flee from—a bizarre symptom of the condition. Behavioral and cognitive therapy are the common means of treatment for amnesiphobia; surgical intervention is usually not encouraged. Ironically, should the amnesiphobe develop the condition that they fear the most, they won't be able to remember that they feared it in the first place.

THINGS TO AVOID: the aging process; getting drunk; football, concussions, and head injuries.

||||| Phobia Trivia |||||

There are two types of amnesia: anterograde amnesia is an inability to form new memories, while retrograde amnesia is the inability to recall past events. Amnesiphobia is commonly related to the development of Alzheimer's disease.

||||| Statistics |||||

New brain connections are created every time you form a new memory, although experts believe that you can hold seven items in short-term memory for only 20 to 30 seconds.

Anemophobia

MEANING: fear of wind

ORIGIN: the Greek word *anemo*, meaning "air" or "wind"

Also known as ancraophobia, ANEMOPHOBIA is the extreme fear of wind or drafts. Commonly caused by a past trauma, such as wind-related property damage, a barbecue getting completely ruined by the wind, or having experienced extreme weather where there was a genuine threat of injury or death, it is also caused by an intense dislike of the feeling or sound of wind. Anemophobes usually avoid wind whenever they can, refusing to leave the house if they detect even the slightest breeze blowing. They are fearful of changes in the weather that indicate an oncoming storm, and they steer clear of things that remind them of the wind, like ocean waves. Even mildly windy days can cause sufferers to experience rapid breathing, tremors, and a feeling of detachment. In addition to hypnotherapy, the primary method of treatment is exposure therapy, which involves sufferers initially standing in front of a fan (on the lowest setting) before working up to standing in a light draft and eventually facing some actual wind. Passing wind, particularly for those who also suffer flatulophobia (the fear of farting), is not recommended in the early stages of this treatment.

THINGS TO AVOID: leaving the house; most mountains and high places; the beach; kite-flying events; Chicago; Wellington, New Zealand; wind farms; the Big Bad Wolf.

|||| Phobia Trivia ||||

Anemophobia is related to aeroacrophobia (the fear of open high places), aerophobia (the fear of air), and lilapsophobia (the fear of tornadoes and hurricanes).

|||| Statistics ||||

The world's windiest city is Wellington, New Zealand. Each year it has an average of 22 days with wind speed above 46 miles per hour and 173 days above 36 miles per hour.

Anthophobia

MEANING: fear of flowers

ORIGIN: the Greek word *anthos*, meaning "flower"

ANTHOPHOBIA is the intense and persistent fear of flowers. While sufferers generally understand that flowers pose no genuine threat, they still experience great anxiety at the sight or thought of flowers of any genus or species, including any part of a flower, such as a petal or stem. While many people find flowers beautiful, antho-

phobes find them really scary. A negative flower-related event is a common cause, such as getting stung by a bee while standing near a flower, as is the association of flowers with funerals and sadness. Seeing someone else get injured (or merely pricked) by the thorn of a rose in a flower-arranging incident gone wrong can cause the phobia, as can seasonal allergies. Those who believe in tarot readings know that the Grim Reaper carries a white rose, and this too can give rise to anthophobia. Sweating, nausea, and a sense of impending doom accompany this condition; sufferers often avoid events where flowers are likely to be present, such as weddings and funerals. Going to picnics and gardens, or going outside at all, can induce crippling fear in extreme anthophobes, compounded by the ridicule—rather than sympathy—received from family and friends. Psychotherapy is the most common treatment, with medication seldom needed for this incredibly rare phobia that only affects a handful of people worldwide.

THINGS TO AVOID: gardens; birthdays; anniversaries; funerals; weddings; flower shops; flower arranging; stopping to smell the roses; Berkeley, California, in the 1960s.

|||| Phobia Trivia ||||

Anthophobia is often confused with the fear of nature, but anthophobes fear only flowers and not all trees and plants (that said, trees and plants that flower can be a source of angst). The Flower Power movement originated in Berkeley, California, in protest of the Vietnam War. American Beat poet Allen Ginsberg coined the expression in 1965 in his essay "How to Make a March/Spectacle." The essay encouraged protesters to hand flowers out to spectators, journalists, and police at anti-war rallies to combat anger, fear, and threat. He must have been banking on the fact that anthophobia is a very rare condition.

|||| Statistics ||||

It is estimated that there are more than 400,000 types of flowering plant species in the world. The world's largest flower is the corpse lily, which grows to a diameter of around 3 feet.

Anthropophobia

MEANING: fear of people

ORIGIN: the Greek word *anthropos*, meaning "man"

ANTHROPOPHOBIA is the fear of people or society. This condition goes beyond the common anxiety around crowded situations and extends to extreme discomfort even in the presence of one other person. While this phobia may arise from a traumatic experience at the hands of another person, it generally stems from an excessive shyness or timidity and tends to develop in high-strung, overanxious individuals. Anthropophobes shut themselves away and avoid direct human contact, limiting social interactions to the written form. If they do come within range of another person, the sufferer avoids eye contact, blushes, doesn't speak, and often feels an overwhelming desire to flee, even from close friends and relatives. Naturally, the idea of starting a relationship is an untenable prospect for the average anthropophobe. Given the vast numbers of people in virtually all parts of the world, life can be rather tough for sufferers of this condition. One realistic solution is to join a remote Amazonian tribe with only a few hundred members, which is surely less stressful than trying to avoid the other 7.5 billion people in the world.

THINGS TO AVOID: the 7.5 billion people that inhabit the Earth; leaving your house; the other people in your house.

||||| Phobia Trivia |||||

The current average population increase is estimated at around 83 million people per year, making life harder and harder for the anthropophobe as the years go on. There are an estimated 100 uncontacted tribes living in complete solitude around the world, many in the densely forested areas of South America. These tribes usually only comprise up to 200 people, so would be ideal for the anthropophobe to join (if you can find one).

It is estimated that between 2 and 7 percent of Americans suffer from some sort of social anxiety disorder.

Anuptaphobia

MEANING: fear of staying single

ORIGIN: the Latin word *nuptialis*, meaning "pertaining to marriage"

ANUPTAPHOBIA is the fear of staying single, that is, alone and not in a relationship. Traditional society places a heavy emphasis on finding a partner and having children. This feeling that success is measured by these factors can lead to anuptaphobia. A lack of self-esteem, a bad breakup or rejection, and childhood abandonment can also cause this phobia. Sufferers tend to be very emotionally dependent and experience extreme anxiety at the thought of being single, petrified that they will never find someone. This can lead to indiscriminate sexual encounters, selecting partners on a whim, or marrying too quickly without considering the implications. An anuptaphobe might also choose to stay in a bad, loveless, or abusive relationship rather than being single. Sufferers can't stand being alone and pursue activities and social interactions with the prospect of meeting a partner. While they hope for the perfect partner with whom to share their life, in the absence of perfection, pretty much anyone will do, because apart from having nobody to snuggle up with in front of the television, nothing is worse than having to constantly take "selfies" (known, as of now, as selfiphobia).

THINGS TO AVOID: staying in on a Friday and Saturday night; a limited social life; being single on Valentine's Day.

||||| Phobia Trivia |||||

Anuptaphobia is related to (and perhaps the opposite of) gamophobia, the fear of marriage.

||||| Statistics |||||

The U.S. Census Bureau estimated that there were 110.6 million unmarried American adults as of 2017. That is 45.2 percent of the adult population, compared with 28 percent in 1960.

Apeirophobia

MEANING: fear of infinity

ORIGIN: the Greek word *apeiros*, meaning "infinite" or "boundless"

APEIROPHOBIA is the extreme fear of infinity or eternity, and everlasting things. Apeirophobia is very complex, and a number of factors can play a role in its cause. The concept is usually linked with death and the afterlife; a child, for example, may have been told that his dead grandmother is now sleeping "eternally." The difficulty of grappling with this notion may contribute to the condition. Science fiction films, television shows, and books that depict vampires, fairies, and magical creatures that live forever can also cause the phobia, as can a genetic predisposition. The concept of infinity or timelessness is a heavy burden for the apeirophobe; sufferers often strive to make their lives as predictable as possible. The idea of waiting or living for eternity can cause thoughts of death, a detachment from reality, depression, and even suicide, especially at night when fearful thoughts are usually intensified. This can impact personal relationships when the sufferer avoids all situations in which they might have to consider the concept. Treating apeirophobia can be difficult; meditation and breathing techniques have some success. Talk therapy can also help educate the patient to take things one day at a time, and understand that nobody lives forever. Knowing that you will inevitably die often provides some much-needed comfort.

THINGS TO AVOID: the letter 8 (if you're lying on your side); eternal salvation; math classes that deal with the concept of infinity; the Bible; *Peter Pan* (books and films).

|||| Phobia Trivia ||||

Paradoxically, apeirophobia is often connected with thanatophobia, the fear of dying, since many sufferers believe that death is followed by an eternal afterlife.

|||| Statistics ||||

The size of infinities can vary. The smallest infinity is how many whole numbers there are, but if fractions are included, there are infinitely more numbers as there are infinitely many fractions between each whole number. Make sense?

Apotemnophobia

MEANING: fear of amputees

ORIGIN: the Greek word *apotemnein*, meaning "cut"

APOTEMNOPHOBIA is the pathological fear of amputees. Often rooted in a past experience, like an injury or witnessing the effects of amputation on someone else, it can also arise from media reports involving amputees from incidents like sporting mishaps. In childhood, it can stem from seeing a person missing a limb, a sight that could be scary or unexpected for a child. The discomforting sense of something missing can cause massive dread in apotemnophobes, resulting in severe unease, panic, and an extreme desire to flee the situation. In most cases, the condition can be treated with behavioral and cognitive therapy, as well as education that amputees are people like the rest of us, there is nothing to fear, and that if you do flee, in most instances (with the exceptions of Steve Austin and the Blade Runner), they are unlikely to catch you.

THINGS TO AVOID: hospitals; the Paralympics; *The Six Million Dollar Man* television series; the film *Forrest Gump*; the *ER* episode where Dr. Barnett has both legs amputated.

||||| Phobia Trivia |||||

The majority of new amputations occur due to complications of the vascular system, especially from diabetes. The opposite condition is acrotomophilia, which is an attraction toward amputees.

||||| Statistics |||||

There were 2 million amputees in the United States as of 2015.

Arachibutyrophobia

MEANING: fear of peanut butter sticking to the roof of the mouth

ORIGIN: the Greek words *arachi*, meaning "ground nut," and *bouturo*, meaning "butter"

ARACHIBUTYROPHOBIA is the extremely weird, extremely rare, and extremely hard-to-pronounce extreme fear of peanut butter sticking to the roof of the mouth. This strange and complex fear is not the fear of peanut butter itself, but specifically the fear of it sticking to the roof of your mouth. The sensation of having the roof of the mouth coated in something that is difficult to remove can result in feelings of discomfort and lack of control, which can cause the phobia. It is also commonly induced by choking on peanut butter or having seen someone else choke on it. Just the thought can lead to trembling, nausea, and catastrophic feelings of doom, and often results in the sufferer avoiding peanut butter on all levels, from smelling it to tasting it or even thinking about it. The arachibutyrophobe's anxiety around any peanut-buttery situation is especially tragic when they still crave the stuff even while they fear eating it. This can turn a person with an acute case of the condition off peanut butter…permanently. Now, that is truly scary.

THINGS TO AVOID: peanut butter (regardless of any penchant for it); school cafeterias; most American kitchens; Choosy Moms; Reese's candy; televisions commercials in the pre-lunchtime hours.

A classic American staple, peanut butter and jelly sandwiches became famous during World War II when soldiers were given them for complete nutrition. Some suggest that the phobia was invented for comedic reasons by Charles M. Schulz in his comic strip *Peanuts*, but it was actually coined by author Peter O'Donnell in his 1985 novel *Dead Man's Handle*, and from there, well, it just spread. The CTRN Phobia Clinic provides "guaranteed lifetime elimination of Sticky Peanut Butter Phobia" for just $1,497, so there is a way out from this debilitating illness.

|||| Statistics ||||

According to the National Peanut Board, it takes about 540 peanuts to make a 12-ounce jar of peanut butter, and to be labeled as such in the U.S., it must be at least 90 percent peanuts. It has been estimated that the average American schoolkid eats around 1,500 PB&J sandwiches by graduation.

Arachnophobia

MEANING: fear of spiders

ORIGIN: the Greek word *arachni*, meaning "spider"

Also spelled "arachnephobia," ARACHNOPHOBIA is the unreasonable fear of spiders, which can extend to other arachnids, such as scorpions. While it is common to be scared of some spiders, sufferers of the phobia are terrified of even the smallest spiders and have extreme anxiety (including heart palpitations, crying, screaming, sweating, and jumping from moving cars) at the sight or thought of these nefarious creatures. Arachnophobes can experience a sense of impending doom if they find themselves in the vicinity of any area they believe could harbor spiders—like gardens, wooded areas, closets, or shoes—even seeing a spider web is too much for many sufferers. Regular home fumigation is often practiced by some arachnophobes. While many scientists believe that arachnophobia is an evolutionary trait—passed down from our ancestors who reduced the risk of being bitten and killed by avoiding spiders—others believe the fear of spiders may be cultural and caused by negative media depictions. As evidence for this, the phobia is far more common in Western society, while some communities in Papua New Guinea, Cambodia, and Chile include spiders in their diet (arachnophobes are advised to avoid dining in these areas). Treatment is typically by exposure therapy, where the sufferer is initially presented with pictures of spiders before being subjected to actual spiders (it is not recommended that the Sydney funnel-web or Goliath bird-eating spider be used for this purpose in the early stages). Medication is also used in cases where the fear renders the person completely dysfunctional.

THINGS TO AVOID: *Spider-Man* films, comic books, and cartoons; Sydney, Australia (see Phobia Trivia on next page); Venezuela (see Phobia Trivia on next page); the nursery rhyme "Little Miss Muffett"; the 1990 film *Arachnophobia*, in which a new species of deadly spider begins killing the residents of a town one by one.

||||| Phobia Trivia |||||

The world's deadliest spider is the Sydney funnel-web spider, with the male's venom being particularly lethal (don't worry too much about the female funnel-webs, as they are nowhere near as deadly as the males). The world's largest spider is the male Goliath bird-eating spider from Venezuela, which has a leg-span of 11 inches, sufficient to cover a dinner plate (again, don't worry too much, as their lifespan is only 10 years). Justin Timberlake has an acute fear of spiders—maybe that's how they make him constantly dance around in his music videos.

||||| Statistics |||||

Arachnophobia is quite a common phobia and afflicts women four times more than men (48 percent of women are affected, compared with 12 percent of men). There is, however, not a great deal to worry about, as an average of only 6.6 people in the United States die from spider bites each year (eight times as many die from bee and wasp stings—apiphobes take note).

Atychiphobia

MEANING: fear of failure

ORIGIN: the Greek word *atyches*, meaning "unfortunate"

ATYCHIPHOBIA is the fear of failure or defeat. While most people experience anxiety or doubt regarding success in any endeavor, atychiphobes often have an extreme lack of confidence in their abilities that results in a fear of ridicule over their failure. An embarrassing event, or strict and overly demanding parents, can also lead to this condition; the sufferer's genetics can play a role as well—those with parents who fear failure are far more likely to fear it themselves. Many atychiphobes refuse to play games or begin tasks unless they are guaranteed success or perfection, and often have unrealistically high expectations, avoiding anything that is unlikely to have a favorable outcome. Sufferers commonly give up on projects, relationships, education, and jobs to avoid failure. They fake illnesses, tell lies, and make excuses, effectively sabotaging their own lives. The worry that an atychiphobe experiences at the thought of competing or completing a task can result in sleeplessness, headaches, gastrointestinal distress, and panic attacks. Motivational techniques and psychotherapy are the most common methods of treatment, helping sufferers view failure as a learning experience. As the great American inventor Thomas Edison once said, "I have not failed. I've just found 10,000 ways that won't work."

THINGS TO AVOID: competing; trying anything at all for the first time; any form of educational examination; the Saturday *New York Times* crossword puzzle; relationships; jobs.

||||| Phobia Trivia |||||

Atychiphobia is also known as kakorrahaphobia or kakorrhaphiophobia, the Greek word *kako* meaning "bad."

||||| Statistics |||||

An estimated 2 to 5 percent of the American population is affected by atychiphobia.

Aulophobia

MEANING: fear of flutes

ORIGIN: the Greek word *aulo*, meaning "tube" or "pipe"

AULOPHOBIA is the abnormal fear
of flutes. Many sufferers of this rare
condition fear the instrument because
of the sound it makes or the clicking
sound from the buttons. The flute's
appearance can also be a source of fear; its phallic shape is
very off-putting to some sufferers, particularly those who also
have ithyphallophobia (the fear of an erect penis). A traumatic
flute-related incident can also cause this phobia, such as being
beaten with the instrument by a flute-wielding assailant, being
forced to learn it despite knowing that it was a pointless pursuit, or having to endure a long and boring eisteddfod. For
sufferers who regularly find themselves in the presence of
flutes, aulophobia can have a considerable impact on their
quality of life. The mere sight of a flute, and the dread that it
is going to be played, can produce symptoms such as sweating, irregular breathing, nausea, and a desire to flee. Should
someone do you a favor of using their flute or other woodwind
instrument, remember to keep your end of the bargain and
pay them before fleeing in fear. History has shown that these
particular musicians can be a rather vindictive lot.

THINGS TO AVOID: the woodwind section of the orchestra;
The Pied Piper.

Flutes are thought to be the earliest musical instruments; a number of flutes dating to 43,000 years ago have been found in the Swabian Jura region of present-day Germany. A person who plays the flute is known as a flutist or flautist.

|||| Statistics ||||

The world-renowned flutist William Kincaid used a platinum flute that was made in 1939 by the Verne Q. Powell Company. It was auctioned at Christie's in 1986 for $187,000, making it the world's most expensive flute.

Auroraphobia

MEANING: fear of northern lights

ORIGIN: the Latin word *aurora*, meaning "dawn"

AURORAPHOBIA is the irrational fear of the aurora borealis. Commonly known as the northern lights, the aurora borealis is a luminous cascade of colorful lighting effects, appearing as eerie streamers or bands of light in the night sky above the magnetic pole in the Northern Hemisphere. For many people, the aurora is a once-in-a-lifetime spectacle. For those who suffer from auroraphobia, not so much. This debilitating condition tends to afflict those who don't fully grasp the science behind the phenomenon, resulting in feeling a lack of control leading to fear. Sufferers also report feeling very small when looking at the lights, a humbling experience that can turn into fear. Experiencing or thinking about the northern lights can cause an inability to function normally and refusal to venture outside on clear winter nights. Extreme sufferers become reclusive during the long northern winters to avoid exposure to the dreaded lights, leading to a limited social life. Some auroraphobes relocate to avoid the lights. But if you do have an acute case of auroraphobia and decide to move south, you'd better not go too far: The aurora australis, or southern lights, occur in the sky above the magnetic pole in the Southern Hemisphere, and they're just as scary.

THINGS TO AVOID: the magnetic pole in the Northern Hemisphere; looking up at the sky or being out at night; media reports on clear winter's days in that area when there is very little else to report on.

|||| Phobia Trivia ||||

The aurora borealis is caused by solar radiation entering the atmosphere. Electrically charged particles from the sun collide with each other, resulting in the colorful lights. Aurora was the goddess of dawn in Roman mythology, renewing herself every morning and flying across the sky, announcing the arrival of the sun.

|||| Statistics ||||

The aurora borealis can be seen up to 200 nights per year in certain areas, most often from mid-August to mid-April.

Is for Blennophobia

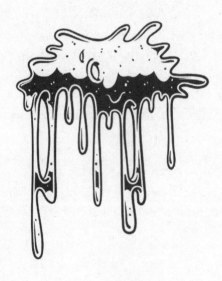

Barophobia

MEANING: fear of gravity

ORIGIN: the Greek word *baros*, meaning "weight"

BAROPHOBIA is the irrational fear of gravity. Sufferers fear that gravity might crush them, that they may fall because of the effects of gravity, or that gravity might cease to exist and they will float away like a balloon in the breeze. A traumatic experience like falling from a great height and getting injured can result in negative associations with gravity that lead to the phobia, as can simply reading a book or watching a film depicting the dire consequences of too much or too little gravity. Learning about the incredible power of gravity as a child can also contribute to the condition. While some sufferers are only slightly uncomfortable at the thought of gravity, others experience extreme anxiety, resulting in heart palpitations, dizziness, and a feeling of being trapped or out of control. Talk therapy is the most common way of treating barophobia, which can be a very debilitating condition, because, unless you go live in space or stuff yourself in a vacuum, gravity is pretty hard to avoid.

THINGS TO AVOID: the Earth; the moon, the sun; planets; stars; black holes (particularly black holes); Isaac Newton.

||||| Phobia Trivia |||||

Black holes have the strongest gravitational fields in the known universe. The gravity of a black hole is so strong that nothing, not even particles or light, can escape from it. Barophobia is closely related to (although distinct from) other phobias such as ambulophobia (the fear of walking), stasibasiphobia or stasiphobia (the fear of standing), bathmophobia (the fear of stairs or steep slopes), and acrophobia (the fear of heights).

Gravity on Earth is far stronger than on the moon, which has 17 percent of Earth's gravity, and on Mars, which has 38 percent of Earth's gravity. That means, with the ability to do a normal run up, a person could long jump around 26 meters (28 yards) on Mars, and as far as 59 meters (65 yards) on the moon.

Batrachophobia

MEANING: fear of amphibians

ORIGIN: the Greek word *batracho*, meaning "frog"

BATRACHOPHOBIA is the intense fear of amphibians including, but not limited to, frogs, toads, newts, and salamanders. While some people find these little animals cute and endearing, batrachophobes will go to extreme lengths to avoid them. The fear has roots in the common myth that touching frogs and toads can cause warts, the belief that they were once used in witchcraft, and that frogs are a bad omen. There is also the concern that some amphibians may be poisonous (and some of them are, most notably the Australian cane toad, which has no natural predators), and their excellent camouflage and quick movement can indeed be pretty scary. Batrachophobia can also arise from seeing one of the diminutive animals die violently, or dissecting a frog in biology class. Childhood pranks, like putting a toad on someone's head or down someone's shirt, are also a common cause of this debilitating fear. Any interaction with amphibians can cause symptoms of panic in the sufferer, who avoids streams, ponds, and outdoor camping areas where frogs and toads generally lurk. Images, frog toys, and even talking about amphibians can trigger nausea, dizziness, and loss of self-control, significantly impacting the sufferer's quality of life. Exposure therapy is the most widely adopted treatment, although the frog-down-the-shirt technique is not recommended. Recovery is generally a long and painstaking process, so for those batrachophobic princesses out there, you might have to wait quite a while before meeting your handsome prince.

THINGS TO AVOID: ponds and other damp environments; French restaurants; *The Muppets.*

IIIII Phobia Trivia IIIII

In one severe case of batrachophobia, recorded in the 1983 *Journal of Behavior Therapy and Experimental Psychiatry,* a woman developed the condition after running over a group of frogs with a lawnmower. The term was first recorded in the 1953 *Psychiatric Dictionary with Encyclopedic Treatment of Modern Terms.* Bufonophobia is the more specific fear of toads, while ranidaphobia is the particular fear of frogs. A group of toads is known as a knot and a group of frogs is an army; perhaps these terms were coined by batrachophobes, because the former causes a knot in the stomach and the latter makes you want an army for protection.

There are approximately 8,000 amphibian species, of which nearly 90 percent are frogs. The world's smallest amphibian is a frog from New Guinea, which has a length of 0.3 inches; the largest is the Chinese giant salamander, at almost 6 feet long.

Blennophobia

MEANING: fear of slime

ORIGIN: the Greek word *blenno*, meaning "mucus"

BLENNOPHOBIA is an extreme and persistent fear of slime and mucus. The offending substances are usually sticky and viscous, like the slime produced by snails or the gel released by some fish. The fear of getting slimed is generally thought to come from a primal subconscious defense mechanism of avoiding slimy mucus or pus-like substances that could cause infection. The phobia is exacerbated by the fact that most slime is sticky in nature, making it difficult and time-consuming to remove from the body and thus intensifying the trauma suffered. The onset of blennophobia can also be caused by a bad slime-related experience or by watching movies with terrifyingly graphic slime-related scenes (see Things to Avoid). These movies are likely to trigger the symptoms of blennophobia, including anxiety, restlessness, sweating, heavy breathing, nervousness, shortness of breath, vomiting, and nausea.

THINGS TO AVOID: snails; slugs; bony fish; hagfish; leeches; snot, phlegm and saliva, especially from someone with a bad cold; the word "phlegmatic"; most gel; the Nickelodeon Kids' Choice Awards; the films *The Blob*, *Alien*, *Poltergeist*, *The Thing*, *Ghostbusters*, *A Nightmare on Elm Street*, *The Toxic Avenger*, *Demons*, *The Fly*, *Street Trash*, *Ghostbusters 2*, *Troll2*, *Home Alone 2: Lost in New York*, *Mighty Morphin Power Rangers: The Movie*, *Batman & Robin*, *Men in Black*, *The Matrix*, *Evolution*, *Pirates of the Caribbean: Dead Man's Chest*, *The Watch*, and *Ghostbusters* (2016 version), among others.

Phobia Trivia

A fear of slime is also known as myxophobia. Snails, slugs, bony fish, and hagfish all produce external mucus. This acts as a protection against both infections and predators, facilitates movement, and plays a role in communication.

Statistics

Slime seems to be of particular fascination to children. Twelve-year-old Maddie Rae holds a place in *Guinness World Records* for creating the world's largest slime, which weighed 6 tons, while 10-year-old Ciela Villa has the record for the longest distance stretching homemade slime in 30 seconds, which was over 7 feet.

Is for Coulrophobia

Catagelophobia

MEANING: fear of being ridiculed

ORIGIN: the Greek words *cara*, meaning "put down," and *gelo*, meaning "laugh"

CATAGELOPHOBIA is the fear of being ridiculed or put down. While nobody likes being the butt of a joke, people with this phobia tend to have low self-esteem that takes root in early childhood. Children are emotionally sensitive, and excessive criticism or condemnation can result in catagelophobia. This can persist into adulthood, where the sufferer becomes reclusive and withdrawn, shunning others for fear of being mocked or teased. Extreme sufferers avoid all social contact and will often misinterpret an innocent comment as a slight. Behavioral therapy is the most effective treatment. Learning that criticism is not always a destructive force is helpful. As the American author Norman Vincent Peale said, "The trouble with most of us is that we would rather be ruined by praise than saved by criticism." For the catagelophobe who can't see the positive side of criticism, there's always the slightly less uplifting advice from another American writer, Elbert Hubbard, who said, "To avoid criticism, do nothing, say nothing, and be nothing."

THINGS TO AVOID: comedy clubs; schoolyards; most workplace environments; most friendships; siblings.

|||| Phobia Trivia ||||

Catagelophobia is also spelled "categelophobia" or "katagelophobia." It is closely related to agoraphobia, the fear of crowds, and geliophobia, the fear of laughter.

According to the American Society for the Positive Care of Children, nearly 30 percent of students ages 12 to 18 are victims of bullying on school grounds at some point.

Catoptrophobia

MEANING: fear of mirrors

ORIGIN: the Greek word *catropto*, meaning "mirror"

Sometimes known as spectrophobia, CATOPTROPHOBIA is the fear of mirrors. Some superstitious sufferers believe they have seen ghosts or apparitions in mirrors, or have a feeling that something might jump out of the mirror or that they are being watched through a mirror. Others fear that mirrors are a gateway into a preternatural world, and that they could be pulled into the mirror by an alien force. Fears can be compounded by horror films and books depicting mirror-related trauma or evil spirits trapped inside mirrors. Sufferers of catoptrophobia avoid looking at themselves in the mirror; even the thought of doing so results in trembling, sweating, and thoughts of dying. Some catoptrophobes even feel anxious at seeing their reflection in silverware or in a body of water (Narcissus from Greek mythology clearly was not afflicted in this way). In addition to relaxation techniques or support groups, the most effective way of treating this phobia is gradual exposure therapy, starting with looking at images of mirrors before finally daring to take a peek into a real one. Best not to try this when you've just gotten out of bed—if the mirror tells you something you don't want to hear, like one does to the witch in *Snow White*, you might actually break it. That means seven years of bad luck.

THINGS TO AVOID: most houses; Versailles; hotel lobbies and bathrooms; looking behind the bar in bars; the 2008 horror film *Mirrors*; *Snow White and the Seven Dwarfs* (books and films).

||||| Phobia Trivia |||||

Catoptrophobia is distinct from eisoptrophobia, which is the fear of one's own reflection. It is a common superstition that if you break a mirror you will receive seven years' bad luck. The ancient Romans believed that a mirror possessed supernatural properties and had the power to confiscate part of a person's soul. Cracking or shattering the mirror, distorting the person's image, could lead to corruption of the soul or getting the soul trapped inside the mirror. It was believed that the damaged soul was less capable of warding off evil spirits and protecting the person from misfortune, thereby making it more likely that they would suffer bad luck. Others believed that the damaged soul itself brought the bad luck, as a punishment for breaking the mirror. But don't fear: If a mirror is broken, there are a number of ways to prevent bad luck. The fragments can be ground up into a fine powder and buried, which destroys the distorted reflection, restoring the soul to the person who broke the mirror. Throwing salt over one's shoulder is another supposed remedy. Some African cultures immerse the broken pieces in a southern-flowing river to remove the bad luck. Burning the pieces of the mirror is also thought to work, as is taking a piece of the mirror and touching it to a tombstone. *Baywatch* star Pamela Anderson has catoptrophobia. Makes you wonder how her hair and makeup are always so neat.

The Hall of Mirrors in Versailles is a room that is 240 feet long and 34 feet wide. On one wall there are 357 mirrors that stretch from floor to ceiling—not the ideal place for catoptrophobes.

Cenosillicaphobia

MEANING: fear of an empty beer glass

ORIGIN: the Greek word *kenos*, meaning "empty," and the Latin word *silix*, meaning "hard stone or flint"

CENOSILLICAPHOBIA is the extreme fear of an empty beer glass. Many people suffer from this debilitating fear, most of them men, and nearly all of them beer drinkers. Borne out of a thirst for beer, which tends to increase as more beer is consumed, cenosillicaphobia can be caused by a traumatic experience, like being unable to get a refill because of an inattentive bartender. For sufferers of this condition, the mere thought of an empty glass results in heart palpitations, a feeling of being trapped or out of control, and an uncomfortably dry mouth. Frustration, anger, and an outright panic attack can also result. The cenosillicaphobe goes to extreme lengths to avoid refill lag time, sitting as close to the bar as possible and giving large tips to the bartender to ensure vigilance is maintained. Luckily, a cure for this debilitating phobia is as close as the nearest keg, bottle, or can, and is easily treated by a good bartender who recognizes the symptoms of cenosillicaphobia and knows how to keep 'em coming. Symptoms of nausea, dizziness, and an inability to think or speak clearly may continue after the glass has been refilled.

THINGS TO AVOID: busy bars; sporting events where refills can be slow to come; drinking the last mouthful too hastily.

Niels Bohr was a Danish Nobel Prize–winning physicist who specialized in quantum theory and atomic structure. The Carlsberg brewery had a passion for science as part of its company culture, so for his efforts Bohr was gifted a house that was located next to the brewery. Bohr was able to drink free beer whenever he wanted as the house had a direct pipeline to the brewery. Bohr stayed there from 1932 until his death in 1962. It is unknown whether Niels Bohr was a cenosillicaphobe or not.

||||| Statistics |||||

The Czechs are the world's biggest beer drinkers, topping the tables for the last 24 consecutive years. In 2016 they drank 287 pints per person, or one every 30 hours. Given that children are unlikely to contribute much to those statistics, the average Czech beer drinker probably drinks a lot more than that. Other front-running countries include Austria, Germany, Poland, and Ireland.

Chaetophobia

MEANING: fear of hair

ORIGIN: the Greek word *khaite*, meaning "loose, flowing hair"

CHAETOPHOBIA is a rare phobia that causes an irrational fear of hair. While many people spend a lot of money and time grooming and looking after their hair, chaetophobes want nothing to do with it. This fear is rooted in the perception that hair is dirty and harbors oil, dandruff, lice, and fungal infections. Sufferers of the phobia are disgusted by hair, fearing that the germs it contains will make them sick. Germaphobia (a fear of germs) is likely to lead to chaetophobia, as is obsessive-compulsive disorder. Hair loss and a fear of going bald can also trigger the  phobia, as can a traumatic experience involving a hirsute person. The symptoms of chaetophobia range from queasiness and shivering to a feeling of detachment and outright panic at the thought of hair. Many chaetophobes are afraid of other people's hair, avoiding in particular those individuals with thick, dense, and curly hairdos. Others do not allow people to touch their hair and keep their hair as clean as possible by shampooing and bathing several times a day. In more extreme cases, the sufferer becomes obsessed with removing every hair on their body. Some chaetophobes live in fear of finding a stray hair in their food. Others are fearful of animal hair. While a combination of medication and psychotherapy can be used to overcome this potent phobia, sufferers face many difficulties in day-to-day life, given that hair is everywhere and continually growing, making it almost impossible to avoid or eradicate.

THINGS TO AVOID: barber shops and hairdressers; more than 99 percent of the world's population; yourself; nearly all animals.

There are a number of very closely related hair fears. Trichopathophobia is the fear of hair disease, from the Greek words *tricho*, meaning "hair," and *patho*, meaning "disease." Trichophobia is the general fear of loose hairs.

The world's longest hair belongs to Xie Qiuping of China, whose hair is over 18 feet long. She has been growing her hair since 1973, when she was 13. Ms. Qiuping is clearly not a sufferer of chaetophobia.

Chirophobia

MEANING: fear of hands

ORIGIN: the Greek word *chiro*, meaning "hand"

CHIROPHOBIA is the fear of hands, either the sufferer's own hands or those of others. This rare phobia generally occurs in response to a traumatic experience, like a bout of severe arthritis or a painful hand injury. The resulting pain and suffering can contribute to a negative attitude toward hands, sometimes leading to chirophobia. Sufferers of this condition are often afraid to wash their hands, and can be seen wearing mittens or gloves as a form of protection. They generally don't like the thought of other people's hands either, and will avoid shaking hands and clapping. Extreme chirophobes will do whatever they can to avoid using their hands, making it difficult to open doors, drive a car, get dressed, wash, or eat. As for how the chirophobe deals with going to the bathroom, well, that's anyone's guess.

THINGS TO AVOID: shaking hands; using your hands; hand modeling; waving; clapping; massages; chiropractors; "The Puffy Shirt" episode of *Seinfeld*.

|||| Phobia Trivia ||||

Chiro in "chiropractor" has the same origin as it does in "chirophobia." The world's most successful, yet largely unheard of, hand model is the American Ashley Covington. While obviously not a chirophobe herself, she nearly always wears gloves to protect her most prized assets.

|||| Statistics ||||

According to the American Chiropractic Association, there are more than 70,000 chiropractors in the U.S., who treat more than 35 million Americans each year.

Chorophobia

MEANING: fear of dancing

ORIGIN: the Greek word *choro*, meaning "dance"

CHOROPHOBIA is the extreme aversion to dancing, or the fear of any event, situation, or person that relates to dancing of any kind. It can arise from a traumatic dance experience, including a disastrous or humiliating public performance. Watching somebody else dance, seeing dancing moves on television, or even thinking about dancing can result in a shortness of breath, sweating, and panic. Actual participation is completely out of the question; chorophobes avoid all places where dancing is likely to take place. Therapy or hypnosis are common treatments, as is addressing inadequate dancing skills with private dance classes, which can improve the condition tremendously. Unsurprisingly, chorophobia is extremely common in men, although it can sometimes be temporarily cured by the consumption of copious amounts of alcohol.

THINGS TO AVOID: nightclubs; music videos; the ballet; weddings; prom; the films *Dirty Dancing* and *Footloose;* nearly all music television channels; *Dancing with the Stars*.

Phobia Trivia

Chorophobia is usually associated with other social phobias, particularly enochlophobia (the fear of crowds). While the band Scissor Sisters claim to have a dancing aversion in their song "I Don't Feel Like Dancin'," the band members' vigorous dancing in the video suggests that they were not feeling chorophobic.

Statistics

In 1518, a dancing plague swept Alsace (now France). In a case of dancing mania, about 400 people were compelled to dance in the streets for days on end. Over a period of one month, some of the dancers collapsed and even died from exhaustion.

Chrometophobia

MEANING: fear of money

ORIGIN: the Greek word *chrimata*, meaning "money"

Also spelled "chrematophobia," CHROMETOPHOBIA is the irrational fear of money. Many people spend their entire lives in the quest to earn more money, but chrometophobes fear any contact with it. This paradoxical condition afflicts those with very little money, including homeless people who would rather starve than beg for money. It can also result from the pressures of managing money and the associated responsibilities, or from negative associations with parents squabbling over money. While some people fear physical money because of a concern for germs, most chrometophobes fear the value of money and dealing with its exchange. This has far-reaching implications for acute sufferers who go so far as to refuse credit card transactions and electronic transfers. Shopping, working, traveling, paying household bills, and other everyday activities become extremely hard, resulting in irrational behavior, social withdrawal, and depression. Mere existence for the chrometophobe becomes almost impossible, and the condition is very hard to cure. One treatment method is to undertake charity work to illustrate the positive side of money and reduce the associations with greed, corruption, the root of all evil, the misfortune that befell King Midas, and the terrible time Richard Pryor's character had in *Brewster's Millions*.

THINGS TO AVOID: monetary notes; monetary coins; credit cards; online banking; capitalism; banks; ATMs; surviving in the developed world.

Historians believe that metal objects were first used as money as early as 5000 BC, although the Lydians (in present-day Turkey) were the first to use coins as money in around 700 BC. The largest bill ever printed in the U.S. was the $100,000 bill.

A 2015 report by the American Psychological Association found that money is the top source of stress; 72 percent of Americans feel anxious about it at least some of the time.

Chronomentrophobia

MEANING: fear of clocks

ORIGIN: the Greek word *chrono*, meaning "time"

CHRONOMENTROPHOBIA is the irrational fear of clocks, which usually extends to watches. People who face strict deadlines or have to punch a clock for work—or are otherwise bound to rigorous punctuality, demanding agendas, or onerous scheduling—often suffer from this phobia. A fear of clocks may arise from underlying thanatophobia (fear of death), as clocks symbolize the passing of time. Chronomentrophobes may feel that clocks control their lives. They usually have an aversion to traditionally shaped clocks or watches with ticking hands, and will instead check the time using a cell phone or computer. The mere sight or sound of a ticking clock can cause depression and anxiety. People with this fear avoid clocks at all costs, which can make life terribly difficult, as clocks appear in bus and train stations, shops, and many other public places. In addition to psychotherapy, dealing with chronomentrophobia takes patience and, ironically, time. If you are a sufferer who happens to have a time machine (one that does not feature a clock prominently), your best bet is to travel to 18th-century England, where chronomentrophobes were able to walk with unrestrained abandon in the largely clock-free landscape (see Phobia Trivia below).

THINGS TO AVOID: clocks; watches; most people's houses; most offices and workplaces; public squares; the crocodile in *Peter Pan;* Big Ben; train stations; airports; the Outkast song "Chronomentrophobia."

|||| Phobia Trivia ||||

Sufferers of chronomentrophobia often have the closely related chronophobia, which is the fear of time. Chronomentrophobia was rife in England in the late 1700s. In 1797, the Duties on Clocks and Watches Act was passed. Known as the "Clock Tax," the act declared that a five-shilling tax would be imposed on every clock or watch in Britain. Many clock owners either hid or got rid of their clocks in order to avoid the tax. Sensing an opportunity, tavern owners hung large clocks on their walls, and anyone who wanted to know the time (and was not scared of clocks) would have to come in. Tavern owners did not mind paying the tax, because people who came in to find out the time were then compelled to purchase a drink. Time-seekers would frequently stay longer than planned, thus they "bought time," which is how that expression originated.

The largest clock in the world is at the Abraj Al-Bait building in Mecca, which has a clock face 141 feet in diameter.

Cibophobia

MEANING: fear of food

ORIGIN: the Latin word *cibus*, meaning "food"

CIBOPHOBIA is the excessive fear of food. This rare and problematic condition often stems from a choking or vomiting episode, or from an unpleasant experience eating spoiled food or getting food poisoning. Some cases of cibophobia are limited to specific foods, but other cibophobes fear all foodstuffs, terrified that the germs lurking in food will make them sick. Cibophobia can turn into an obsession with expiration dates and how food is cooked, refusal to eat in restaurants or anywhere outside the home, or a tendency to eat as little as possible. This can lead to nutritional deficiencies and other health problems, as well as temper tantrums and behavioral issues in children. Because food is essential to human survival, early treatment of this condition is important, and may involve exposure therapy, psychotherapy, and relaxation techniques using soothing music—just be sure that the soundtrack to *Oliver!* with the song "Food, Glorious Food" doesn't get played.

THINGS TO AVOID: food, and the places that serve it.

Fear of food is also known as sitophobia or sitiophobia, which is from the Greek word *sitos*, meaning "wheat or bread." Cibophobia may be related to emetophobia, which is the fear of vomiting. Cibophobia is often mistaken for anorexia or other eating disorders, but is a separate condition.

Humans are able to survive for around 30 to 40 days without food—Mahatma Gandhi's longest hunger strike lasted for 21 days.

Consecotaleophobia

MEANING: fear of chopsticks

ORIGIN: the Latin word *consecare*, meaning "to cut into pieces" or "chop up"

CONSECOTALEOPHOBIA is the extreme fear of chopsticks. While eating with chopsticks can be challenging for many Western diners, consecotaleophobes are terrified of it. This fear commonly arises from how difficult it is to use the two small sticks. Some might have had a bad experience using chopsticks that prevented them from enjoying their meal. Symptoms include dizziness and breathlessness, especially if the episode occurred when the person was particularly hungry. The messiness associated with poor chopstick technique can also trigger consecotaleophobia in people with obsessive-compulsive disorder. Racism can also play a role in those who dislike Asian countries. Sufferers of this condition will do their utmost to avoid eating at Chinese, Japanese, Korean, and other Asian restaurants, or will insist on using silverware instead of chopsticks. In addition to behavioral and cognitive therapy, practice can go a long way to mitigating the deleterious symptoms of this phobia so that sufferers can eventually go on to lead fairly normal lives. But even in successfully treated cases, there is still the very real fear of getting a bad splinter.

THINGS TO AVOID: sushi; dim sum; most of Asia; games of pool while under the influence of hallucinogenic drugs.

Phobia Trivia

It is believed that chopsticks were invented about 9,000 years ago as a cooking utensil, and that it wasn't until around 1300, during the Ming dynasty, that they were used for eating. There are a number of taboos surrounding chopsticks: You shouldn't stretch your index finger along the chopstick, as this can be interpreted as an accusation; it is considered poor manners to suck the ends of chopsticks; and don't insert chopsticks vertically into the bowl—this is done only when burning incense as a sacrifice to the dead. Consecotaleophobia is related to sinophobia (the fear of China or Chinese culture) and Japanophobia (the fear of Japan or Japanese culture).

Statistics

The most widespread use of disposable chopsticks is in Japan and China. The Japanese use a total of 24 billion pairs each year, while the Chinese use 45 billion pairs each year—certainly not places for consecotaleophobes to venture.

Coprastasophobia

MEANING: fear of constipation

ORIGIN: the Greek word *kopro*, meaning "feces," and the Latin word *sta*, meaning "fixed"

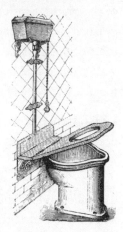

COPRASTASOPHOBIA is the irrational fear of constipation or, more specifically, the fear of becoming constipated. For coprastasophobes, being "stopped up" is their greatest fear. This phobia can result from a medical condition like irritable bowel syndrome, or a particularly discomforting bout of constipation. Vanity can also play a part in the development of coprastasophobia. Worry over weight gain or the desire to avoid unattractive bloating can lead to the fear. Headaches, panic attacks, and a sense of impending doom accompany the phobia; many coprastasophobes avoid certain foods and drinks that may reduce bowel movements. Others adopt a diet that is high in fiber and may go to more extreme lengths, such as laxative abuse, in order to remain regular. Enemas are also employed by some more desperate sufferers. Education about nutrition and healthy eating is the most effective treatment for the condition; hypnosis has also proven successful.

THINGS TO AVOID: low-fiber diets; the *Seinfeld* episode "The Pilot" where Kramer gets badly constipated.

||||| Phobia Trivia |||||

Considered by some to be the opposite of coprastasophobia, coprophobia is the fear of feces or defecation.

According to the National Institute of Diabetes and Digestive and Kidney Diseases, around 42 million Americans are regularly constipated. It is unknown how many of these are actually coprastasophobes, but it likely that very few enjoy it.

Coulrophobia

MEANING: fear of clowns

ORIGIN: the Greek word *kolon*, meaning "limb" in the sense of "stilt walker"

COULROPHOBIA is an irrational and persistent fear of clowns; sufferers feel traumatized at the thought of them and panic-stricken at the sight. The term was coined in the 1980s, but psychologists believe that the fear could be rooted in early childhood, when children are highly sensitive to unfamiliar faces in familiar bodies. A clown's unnatural and distorted features make some people feel threatened and unsafe. Not knowing the identity of the person behind the red nose, white face, and crazy hair adds to the coulrophobe's unease. Despite the recent recognition of the phenomenon, people have been scared of clowns since medieval times, when court jesters, or "village idiots," were able to mock and blaspheme with joyful abandon. This continued into Shakespearean times with the role of the "fool" appearing in many plays. In recent times, the portrayal of evil clowns in the media has greatly increased the prevalence of the phobia, and it is thought that the 1990 miniseries *It*, based on Stephen King's novel of the same name, is largely to blame—there was just something about that wisecracking clown that scared the life out of people. Coulrophobia is not limited to children. Many adults suffer from the condition, primarily in Western society where clowns are more prevalent. For coulrophobes, clowns are no laughing matter. Fortunately, clowns are easily avoided, so the sufferers of this debilitating condition are usually able to lead fairly normal lives.

THINGS TO AVOID: children's birthday parties; circuses; certain rodeos; *The Simpsons*; McDonald's; little orange, white, and black fish.

|||| Phobia Trivia ||||

The phobia can encompass all clowns and is not merely restricted to so-called evil clowns. In 2014, Glenn Kohlberger, president of America's largest clown club, Clowns of America International, came out in defense of clowns in *The Hollywood Reporter*: "Hollywood makes money sensationalizing the norm. They can take any situation no matter how good or pure and turn it into a nightmare. We do not support in any way, shape, or form any medium that sensationalizes or adds to coulrophobia or "clown fear."

Famous coulrophobes include rap star P. Diddy, *Harry Potter* actor Daniel Radcliffe, and Johnny Depp, whose phobia is the product of childhood nightmares of leering clowns. In a 2014 interview with *The Daily Star*, he said, "It's impossible, thanks to their painted-on smiles, to distinguish if they are happy or if they are about to bite your face off. There always seems to be a darkness lurking just under the surface, a potential for real evil."

It is estimated that around 12 percent of adults in the U.S. are afflicted, although coulrophobia is not listed among the American Psychiatric Association's recognized disorders.

Cucurbitophobia

MEANING: fear of pumpkins

ORIGIN: the Latin word *cucurbita*, meaning "gourd"

CUCURBITOPHOBIA is the excessive and unreasonable fear of pumpkins. This unsurprisingly common phobia is usually related to the association of pumpkins with Halloween. Because of the soft nature of the seasonal squash, the Celts, Irish, and Scots who migrated to America used them to carve jack-o'-lanterns for frightening holiday displays. The hideous faces and flickering internal candles of the carved pumpkins can be a chilling vision, and is often enough to make people with a nervous disposition tremble in utter fear, afraid that the scary squash will come to life and attack them. A childhood trauma related to a carved pumpkin can also result in cucurbitophobia; symptoms include crying, shrieking, trembling, abdominal discomfort, passing out, and a desperate desire to flee the scene. Treatment for this phobia involves pumpkin desensitization, beginning with looking at them, then touching them, and eventually holding them. Teaching the patient that pumpkins are not perilous produce and virtually never come to life (and, were they to, would not have any means to attack) is also beneficial.

THINGS TO AVOID: Halloween; fall traditions like carving jack-o'-lanterns and visiting the pumpkin patch; pumpkin-throwing contests; pumpkin soup; pumpkin pie; Thanksgiving dinner.

|||| Phobia Trivia ||||

The legend of the jack-o'-lantern comes from Ireland, where a very mean man named Jack lived. Upon his death, he was not allowed into heaven and was sent to hell, where he was welcomed. But Jack was so mean that he got kicked out of hell and the devil condemned him to an eternity of wandering the darkness between heaven and hell. After some time, Jack asked the devil to give him some light, so the devil gave him a piece of burning coal. Jack carved out a turnip and put the coal inside to use as light. A related phobia is samhainophobia, the fear of Halloween.

|||| Statistics ||||

Pumpkins have been grown in America for 5,000 years. The largest pumpkin ever was grown in Minnesota in 2010 and weighed over 1,810 pounds. In 2018, the average American spent $185.50 on Halloween.

Cypridophobia

MEANING: fear of sex workers (and venereal disease)

ORIGIN: the Greek word *cypri*, meaning "lewd or licentious woman"

CYPRIDOPHOBIA is the morbid fear of sex workers and venereal diseases. Also spelled "cypriphobia," "cyprianophobia," or "cyprinophobia," the condition often arises when someone contracts a sexually transmitted disease from a sexual liaison. Ridicule suffered at the hands of friends can also cause or exacerbate the phobia. While most sex workers practice safe sex, some don't, and venereal diseases are on the rise. Many cypridophobes avoid going to bars where they might run into sex workers and experience extreme anxiety even at the thought of encountering one. Some sufferers refuse to have sex at all. Treatment of cypridophobia includes cognitive and behavioral therapy, as well as proper education about safe sexual practices. Avoiding triggers that set off the phobia is also beneficial in reducing the cypridophobe's anxiety—staying out of brothels entirely is a good start.

THINGS TO AVOID: sex workers; houses of ill repute; many strip clubs; Western movies; a boys' weekend in Las Vegas; Amsterdam; the movie *Pretty Woman*.

||||| Phobia Trivia |||||

Cypridophobia is related to but distinct from erotophobia (the fear of sex) and coitophobia (the fear of sexual intercourse).

||||| Statistics |||||

According to the Centers for Disease Control and Prevention, rates of syphilis, gonorrhea, and chlamydia in the U.S. climbed for the fourth consecutive year in 2018, with nearly 2.3 million cases diagnosed, breaking the 2016 record by more than 200,000.

Is for
Didaskaleinophobia

Decidophobia

MEANING: fear of making decisions

ORIGIN: the Latin word *decido*, meaning "decision"

DECIDOPHOBIA is the fear of making decisions, especially life-altering decisions or decisions about money. Often caused by a bad childhood experience with decision making, perhaps an unwise decision that led to devastating consequences, it can also arise in adulthood after a sufferer's choices lead to trauma. A lack of self-esteem is common in decidophobes, who fear being responsible for other people, preferring to follow the majority and rely on others to make decisions for them, even when the decidophobe knows that their own idea is a better one. Sufferers can be subservient, looking to teachers, parents, friends, and employers to make decisions, and will exhibit symptoms of intense anxiety when confronted with decisions. In extreme cases, decidophobes fear making even the simplest of decisions about when to eat, drink, talk, sit, or stand. Given that the average person makes thousands of decisions every day, frequently without even thinking about it, treatment for this phobia is essential for a normal life. And besides, nobody likes a fence sitter.

THINGS TO AVOID: being in any position of leadership; generally existing on a day-to-day basis.

|||| Phobia Trivia ||||

The term *decidophobia* was coined by Princeton University philosopher Walter Kaufmann in his 1973 book *Without Guilt and Justice*, which deals with the phenomenon.

It is estimated that the average adult makes around 35,000 decisions each day. Assuming seven hours' sleep per day, that makes about one decision every two seconds. There really is nowhere to hide for decidophobes.

Deipnophobia

MEANING: fear of dinner conversation

ORIGIN: the Greek word *deipno*, meaning "dining"

DEIPNOPHOBIA is the extreme fear of dinner conversation. Many people consider it a very pleasurable experience to be dining out and having conversations with friends. Deipnophobes, on the other hand, despise and fear it. This condition is often borne out of a past traumatic experience, like a forced dinner with an irksome stranger, or a blind date who turned out to be intolerably boring. Losing a job or business opportunity because of your disastrous chitchat can also cause the phobia, as can a childhood devoid of love and lessons on table etiquette. Others fear dinner conversation because of the awkwardness of trying to talk and eat at the same time; the condition is exacerbated in the presence of strangers. Deipnophobes will go to extreme lengths to avoid eating-based social gatherings, freezing at the idea of conversation in the presence of food. Others overcompensate for their fear by trying too hard to converse, thus saying something socially unacceptable and turning their phobia into a self-fulfilling prophecy. Symptoms include trembling, sweating, and panic, leading sufferers to become introverted, unable to date or get married, or eat anywhere but home. Hypnotherapy and neuro-linguistic programming have had some success in treating deipnophobia. While the consumption of copious amounts of alcohol does not necessarily treat the phobia, it can go a long way to mitigating the symptoms, or at least helping the sufferer to forget the traumatic experience.

THINGS TO AVOID: dinners with other people; dinners where anybody is likely to speak.

Phobia Trivia

Deipnophobia is a form of sociophobia, which is the fear of social gatherings, socializing, and embarrassment in social situations.

Statistics

It is estimated that women say around 20,000 words per day, while men say around 7,000. Assuming seven hours are for sleep, that makes it about 1,200 words per hour for women and 400 words per hour for men. At an eight-person dinner party consisting of four men and four women that lasts for three hours, the number of words spoken will be in the vicinity of 19,000. That's a lot for the deipnophobe to avoid.

Dementophobia

MEANING: fear of insanity

ORIGIN: the Greek word *dementos*, meaning "insanity"

Also known as agateophobia (from the Greek *agate*, meaning "insanity") and maniaphobia (from the Greek *mania*, meaning "madness"), DEMENTOPHOBIA is the fear of insanity or of becoming insane. History has shown that society has been very cruel to people suffering from mental disorders, locking them away in asylums where they were treated horribly and given electric shock therapy against their will. People who have witnessed a family member or friend endure such treatment, or who have seen it portrayed in media or in movies, can develop dementophobia. A traumatic experience or stressful situation can also lead to abnormal behavior like losing focus or speaking incoherently, which can make a person fear the possibility of going crazy. Watching famous role models succumb to depression and insanity can also trigger dementophobia. Symptoms include irregular heartbeat, shortness of breath, and feelings of dread that can lead dementophobes to become socially withdrawn and severely depressed, refusing to leave the house and unable to hold down a steady job. In a self-fulfilling prophecy, the dementophobe actually exhibits symptoms of insanity, eventually becoming what they fear most. Medication is often used to treat this condition, which, in a catch-22 situation, can actually contribute to the sufferer's fear that they are crazy. In most cases, however, medication is considered better than a lobotomy.

THINGS TO AVOID: mental asylums; *One Flew Over the Cuckoo's Nest* (book and film—definitely avoid this terrifying depiction); Jack Nicholson; the Joseph Heller book *Catch-22*, the basis of which is the Air Force paradox about flying combat missions—if one is crazy, one does not have to fly missions, yet one must be crazy to fly them.

||||| Phobia Trivia |||||

The expression "gone 'round the bend" relates to the placement of mental hospitals. In 19th-century Victorian England, a number of hospitals were built to house the mentally disabled. Long, straight driveways were characteristic of stately homes so that they could be viewed with envy from the street. Conversely, mental asylums were built at the end of long curved driveways, so that they remained unseen from the road. If someone was committed to an asylum, they had literally gone around the bend.

||||| Statistics |||||

According to the World Health Organization, around 50 million people worldwide have dementia.

Dendrophobia

MEANING: fear of trees

ORIGIN: the Greek word *dendro*, meaning "tree"

DENDROPHOBIA is the fear of trees, a phobia that affects an extremely small percentage of the population. Most people find trees to be peaceful and calming, but dendrophobes are petrified of them, some scared of specific trees, while others are scared of all trees. This phobia can come from a traumatic forest-based experience—getting attacked by a creature hiding in the trees, or getting poked in the eye by a low tree branch—but more often relates to the fear of getting hit by a falling tree. Trees can become diseased and hollow, likely to fall at any time, and this unpredictability can lead to dendrophobia. In addition to a rapid pulse and dizziness in the vicinity of trees, sufferers also begin to suspect that even healthy trees look abnormal or threatening. Education that trees are inanimate objects and are not inherently dangerous or intentionally out to harm people is the best form of treatment. In extreme cases, the patient is medicated.

THINGS TO AVOID: forests and woodlands; Colorado; Canada; the reality TV show *Ax Men*; contemplating the "if a tree falls in the forest and nobody is there to hear it, does it actually make a sound?" conundrum.

|||| Phobia Trivia ||||

Dendrophobia is closely related to hylophobia (the fear of forests), xylophobia (the fear of wooden objects and/or forests), and nyctohylophobia (the fear of dark, wooded areas or forests at night). The ancient Druids worshipped trees (oaks in particular) and believed that protective spirits lived within them. Trees, they believed, were sources of good and warded off evil spirits. People in need of good luck would touch a tree, while others actually wore small pieces of oak on necklaces so the wood was always in contact with their skin. In fact, that is the origin of the expression "knock on wood."

The biggest contiguous forest in the world is the Russian taiga, also known as the boreal forest of Russia. It transcends continents, beginning in Europe and extending to the Bering Strait and Pacific Ocean. California's Hyperion redwood is the world's tallest tree, measuring 379 feet. The world's oldest trees are the Great Basin bristlecone pine trees from California and Nevada. They are thought to be over 5,000 years old.

Didaskaleinophobia

MEANING: fear of school

ORIGIN: the Greek word *didasko*, meaning "to teach"

DIDASKALEINOPHOBIA, the fear of school, is a phobia that, unsurprisingly, mainly afflicts kids. Truants who merely skip school because they are bored or rebellious are not actually didaskaleinophobes—they just don't feel like going. Genuine sufferers of the condition may feel nauseated and vomit—or even cry and scream in a full-blown panic attack—at the thought of going to school. The phobia is typically more common in preschool children between four and six years old who also suffer from separation anxiety. An unsafe school environment, bullying, or an increased workload (beginning in late middle school and high school) are other factors that can trigger the phobia. Many educators are aware of this condition, which is acknowledged by the Anxiety Disorders Association of America, so afflicted children should provide a doctor's note that reads "I'm a didaskaleinophobe," and see just how smart their teacher really is.

THINGS TO AVOID: schools and other educational facilities; teachers; homework.

Another term for the fear of school is scholionophobia, which is derived from the Latin word *scius*, meaning "knowing." Some suggest that Mark Twain's famous character Tom Sawyer was a didaskaleinophobe, as he often played hooky from school. Like many kids, however, he did not suffer from the condition, he just had better things to do.

||||| Statistics |||||

Between 2 and 5 percent of children worldwide are known to be afflicted with didaskaleinophobia.

Dikephobia

MEANING: fear of justice

ORIGIN: the Greek word *dik*, meaning "justice"

DIKEPHOBIA is the persistent and overwhelming fear of justice: Sufferers experience anxiety when confronted with anything related to the justice system, including police officers, judges, prison guards, or television programs featuring courtrooms or law enforcement. While many dikephobes have a previous criminal record and do not want to be subjected to the justice system again, some sufferers are law-abiding citizens who go to extreme lengths to avoid breaking the law for fear of the repercussions. This subset exhibit great fear if they commit even the most minor regulatory infraction. A third group of dikephobes believe the justice system is flawed and have a fundamental distrust of the concept. Dikephobia is thought to stem from an unresolved emotional conflict, having something to hide, or a past criminal record. For religious sufferers, the concept of Judgment Day can also be a source of anxiety. The idea of being locked up in jail is absolutely terrifying for dikephobes, but, then again, it's pretty scary for most non-dikephobes too. Counseling has had some success in treating the phobia, but rehabilitation by incarceration, not so much.

THINGS TO AVOID: Judge Judy; Dog the Bounty Hunter; jail; police; courts; judges; lawyers; Themis, the Greek goddess of justice; Batman, Superman, Spider-Man and other superhero vigilantes; *Justice League; Law & Order, NYPD Blue*, and the multitude of other TV procedural dramas.

Phobia Trivia

Notable dikephobes include Billy the Kid, Al Capone, the Joker, mafia members, and motorcycle gangs. The opposite of dikephobia is scelerophobia, the fear of crime.

Statistics

As of 2016, half the world's 9-million-person prison population was held in the U.S., China, and Russia, and the Prison Policy Initiative estimated that 2.3 million people were incarcerated in the U.S., which is around 0.7 percent of the population. That puts the U.S. as having the world's highest prison rate.

Dimanchophobia

MEANING: fear of Sundays

ORIGIN: the Latin word *dimanche*, meaning "Lord's day"

DIMANCHOPHOBIA is the fear of Sundays. Colloquially known as the Sunday Sads or Sunday Scaries, it is a condition that can reflect the fear of unstructured time, but in the majority of cases represents the extreme dread of the impending work or school week (even more severe if accompanied by didaskaleinophobia [the fear of school] or ergophobia [the fear of work]). Dimanchophobia often begins in childhood, especially for victims of bullying or other abuse at school. But it can also begin with adults who find themselves in a soul-destroying job or with a draconian, Mr. Burns–esque boss. These back-to-work (or school) blues associated with the arrival of Monday can make for a horrendous Sunday, resulting in depression and anxiety. Behavioral therapy is often used to treat this condition, while many people resort to the consumption of large quantities of alcohol on Sunday to reduce their fears by forgetting what day it actually is. This self-help technique generally has success; however, it does come with a cost. Being hung over on a Monday morning will certainly make you forget your dimanchophobia, because the onset of lunaediesophobia (the fear of Mondays) will be so overpowering that you won't be able to think of anything else.

THINGS TO AVOID: the day that comes after Saturday; thinking about work or school.

Dimanchophobia is also known as acalendrical anxiety and is distinct from didominicaphobia or kyriakephobia, which is a fear of the Lord's Day for religious reasons.

|||| Statistics ||||

The average American will live through just over 4,100 Sundays in their lifetime, which makes for a lot of avoiding to do if you happen to be a dimanchophobe.

Dishabiliophobia

MEANING: fear of undressing in front of someone

ORIGIN: the Latin words *dis*, meaning "to separate," and *habil*, meaning "clothing"

DISHABILIOPHOBIA is the extreme fear of undressing in front of someone. For many people, undressing in front of someone can be intimidating, but dishabiliophobia affects people with very poor self-esteem and a negative body image. The phobia can develop in people who are ashamed of skin conditions or deformities, and is far more prevalent in women because of society's unrealistic standards for female beauty. Overweight people are more likely to develop dishabiliophobia, especially if they happen to be undressing in front of a cacomorphobe (one who is fearful of obese people). While some sufferers will avoid changing rooms, locker rooms, and even the doctor's office, others will go to the point of avoiding social contact altogether, reluctant to enter into an intimate relationship for fear of having to undress in front of their partner. Support groups and psychotherapy can resolve the dishabiliophobe's fear, but another remedy is simply to turn off the lights before having sex.

THINGS TO AVOID: department store changing rooms; locker rooms; being married; living with people; doctors' offices; schools.

|||| Phobia Trivia ||||

Closely related to dishabiliophobia is gymnophobia (the fear of nudity), although this latter condition doesn't require another person to be present to instill the fear.

|||| Statistics ||||

It is believed that humans began wearing clothing, in the form of animal skins, as far back as 500,000 years ago. Before that period, dishabiliophobia didn't exist and there was presumably only the related gymnophobia.

Disposophobia

MEANING: fear of getting rid of things

ORIGIN: the Latin word *dispos*, meaning "dispose"

DISPOSOPHOBIA is the intense fear of getting rid of things, resulting in hoarding. Also known as hoarding disorder, disposophobia often stems from having thrown something out without realizing its importance, resulting in feelings of intense regret. Feelings of wastefulness can also trigger the phobia, as can the associating of human-like qualities to an object, inspiring guilt or sadness at the thought of throwing it away. People with one of a number of neurological disorders, including schizophrenia, dementia, or obsessive-compulsive disorder, are also more likely to develop disposophobia. Sufferers of this condition tend to save every single thing they acquire, including old magazines, worn-out clothes, newspapers, receipts, and shopping lists. Their houses can be cluttered, with hoarded items stacked in passages and hallways in a disorganized fashion. Most disposophobes display symptoms of extreme anxiety at the thought of throwing out even the most unnecessary of items, often choosing to run away or hide before doing so. Two common forms of disposophobia are book hoarding and animal hoarding. In the latter case, the sufferer often lives in very unsanitary conditions. Disposophobia can have a grave effect on personal and professional relationships; sufferers typically live alone—apart from the piles of boxes and garbage littered throughout the house, that is. And the vermin.

THINGS TO AVOID: garbage bins; garbage trucks; overzealous spouses who throw things out without asking.

|||| Phobia Trivia ||||

The United Kingdom has the highest number of people affected with this condition. The opposite of disposophobia is known as compulsive decluttering.

|||| Statistics ||||

Disposophobia is estimated to exist in around 2 percent of adults worldwide.

Dromophobia

MEANING: fear of crossing the street

ORIGIN: the Greek word *dromos*, meaning "racetrack"

DROMOPHOBIA is the irrational fear of crossing the street, and is usually the result of a past trauma, like getting hit by a car or seeing someone else get hit while crossing the street. This sort of event can result in post-traumatic stress disorder, where sufferers see every car, bus, truck, and motorcycle as a potential threat. Someone with limited mobility or stiff person syndrome (SPS) is more likely to develop dromophobia because of the increased danger for them in crossing the street. Sufferers of this condition may enjoy walking in the park or along a river, but if that stroll entails crossing a street, they are likely to run away in fear, or experience extreme anxiety, vomiting, or difficulty breathing. Some dromophobes isolate themselves, refusing to leave home. Just the thought of crossing the street can cause a panic attack. Counseling is the most common method of treatment—just hope that the therapist doesn't try to break the ice by telling that classic joke:

Q: Why did the dromophobic chicken cross the road?

A: It didn't.

THINGS TO AVOID: cities and towns; the "Why did the chicken cross the road?" joke; the music video for Bruce Springsteen's "Streets of Philadelphia"; the road-running scenes in *Rocky* and *Rocky II*; *Sesame Street*, which is set entirely on a street.

Dromophobia is effectively the same condition as agyrophobia (the fear of streets or crossing the street) and agyiophobia (the fear of busy streets or crossing a busy street).

According to a report by the Governors Highway Safety Association, nearly 6,000 pedestrian deaths occurred in the U.S. in 2017.

Is for
Eleutherophobia

Ecophobia

MEANING: fear of home

ORIGIN: the Greek word *oikos*, meaning "household" or "house"

Also spelled "eicophobia," ECOPHOBIA is the fear of home, or of the contents of a house, including household appliances, furniture, bathtubs, or other objects perceived as potentially dangerous. Also known as oikophobia or domatophobia, this extreme aversion to household surroundings is quite unusual, as most people feel a sense of security when at home. Ecophobia is more common in individuals who have experienced emotional or physical abuse at home, either in the form of domestic violence or at the hands of an intruder. It may also be found in those who think staying at home (particularly those who have never left) is an indicator of failure. Elderly people are at risk of developing this phobia when being at home becomes associated with being alone and lonely, as are people who fear that their house is haunted (this is especially bad for those who are also phasmophobic, or have the fear of ghosts). Ecophobes generally view homes as repressive and unsafe and feel extreme dread when entering a house. Even sounds like creaking floors and shutting doors can elicit sweating, loss of consciousness, tremors, and crying.

THINGS TO AVOID: John Denver's "Take Me Home, Country Roads" and "Back Home Again"; the Tom Jones song "Green, Green Grass of Home"; the Simon & Garfunkel song "Homeward Bound"; many, many other songs describing the joys of home and of going home; any house or place of residence; stories of Baba Yaga, whose house had a mind (and legs!) of its own.

Nostophobia, the fear of returning home, is closely related to ecophobia and is the opposite of nostalgia. Ecophobia has been used to describe a desire (particularly by the English) to leave home and travel, most notably by the 19th-century poet Robert Southey. The term has also been used in a political context to refer to ideologies that repudiate one's own culture and laud others. In the post–World War II era, the term also referred to the fear and loathing of housework experienced by women who had worked outside the home and become more independent during wartime.

According to the Environmental Protection Agency, the average American spent 87 percent of their time in 2018 indoors, the vast majority of that at home.

Eleutherophobia

MEANING: fear of freedom

ORIGIN: the Greek word *eleutheria*, meaning "free"

ELEUTHEROPHOBIA is the fear of freedom (yes, you read that right). According to the Bible, the fear dates back to the time of Moses, when the Israelites became disgruntled at the difficulty of living in the desert and wished to again be slaves to the

Egyptians instead. Indeed, eleutherophobia has sometimes existed among slaves throughout history, with the sufferers feeling that being free entailed more onerous responsibilities and challenges. Eleutherophobes tend to be followers instead of leaders, and derive comfort from being told what to do and not having to think for themselves. Symptoms of eleutherophobia include nausea at the thought of being free, tremors, suspicion of others, and a sense of servitude. Overcoming this fear usually involves therapy and the explanation of what it means to be free and how, if taken one day at a time, it's really not all that scary.

THINGS TO AVOID: most of the world, especially the free part; the Statue of Liberty and all it stands for; the last line of "The Star-Spangled Banner"; the ending of *Braveheart*, where the word is screamed aggressively by Mel Gibson just before his character is disemboweled.

|||| Phobia Trivia ||||

Two famous characters who were most likely eleutherophobes were Red and Brooks from *The Shawshank Redemption* after they became "institutionalized." Nearly all members of the notable revolutions in history (American, French, Russian, etc.) are unlikely to have been eleutherophobes. Eleutheromania (or eleutherophilia) is the frantic zeal for freedom, which is the opposite of eleutherophobia.

|||| Statistics ||||

According to a 2017 study by Freedom in the World, of the 195 countries assessed, 87 were rated as free (45 percent) and 49 as not free (25 percent). The balance were rated as partly free.

Emetophobia

MEANING: fear of vomiting

ORIGIN: the Greek word *emesis*, meaning "an act of vomiting"

EMETOPHOBIA is the fear of vomiting. While vomiting is an unpleasant experience for most people, emetophobes are utterly petrified of it. Though sometimes related to a fear of heights or motion sickness, emetophobia is the specific fear of vomiting regardless of the cause. The fear is generally brought about by a particularly bad bout of vomiting that the person found traumatic, or by being embarrassed after a public vomiting episode. The shame associated with vomiting as a result of parental scolding (and sometimes punishment) as a child can also bring about the condition. Some experts believe that emetophobia may be linked to anxiety over a lack of control, as throwing up is almost impossible to control. This condition can greatly affect the life of the sufferer, who may restrict social activities to avoid any situations involving alcohol or food consumption. They may limit their exposure to children for fear of germs, and women may avoid pregnancy for fear of morning sickness. All forms of travel are also shunned because of the possibility of motion sickness. People with this phobia avoid roller coaster rides and theme parks in general. The anxiety experienced by many emetophobes when they encounter vomit (if they are unable to flee the scene, which is the usual response) can also lead to nausea and vomiting, creating a cyclical problem. And it gets worse: To avoid throwing up, some emetophobes adhere to strict diets, which can lead to cibophobia, the fear of food.

THINGS TO AVOID: excessive alcohol consumption; food that is past its expiration date; roller coasters.

Emetophobia is not limited by age or maturity level, though women generally suffer more than men. This specific phobia also includes a number of subcategories, including the fear of vomiting in public, fear of seeing someone vomit, and fear of seeing vomit itself. Many unlucky emetophobes suffer from all. Famous emetophobes include stand-up comedian Christina Pazsitzky, actress and model Ashley Benson, and actress Denise Richards—perhaps that's the reason she left Charlie Sheen.

||||| Statistics |||||

According to Anxiety U.K., emetophobia is one of the 10 most common phobias in Britain.

Enochlophobia

MEANING: fear of crowds

ORIGIN: the Greek word *ochlo*, meaning "crowd"

Also known as ochlophobia, ENOCHLOPHOBIA is the fear of large crowds or gatherings. Closely related to demophobia, which is the fear of unruly mobs, enochlophobia is relatively common and tends to affect women more than men. It is especially prevalent among people with a shy or introverted disposition, who will go to extreme lengths to avoid large groups of people, often leading to further social isolation. Thought by experts to be the result of genetic or biochemical irregularities in the brain, the onset of the phobia can be caused by a traumatic experience, an intense need for personal space, or a strong dislike of the noise created by a mass of people. The phobia may also result from feelings of insignificance or unimportance when surrounded by a crowd. There is also the fear that the sufferer might contract a deadly disease, get lost in the crowd, or crushed or trampled. The phobia can be extremely debilitating; symptoms range from a feeling of being choked and unable to breathe to trembling, excessive sweating, and blacking out, vastly increasing the likelihood of the sufferer actually being crushed or trampled.

THINGS TO AVOID: Manhattan; Shanghai; sports stadiums; theaters; concerts (and mosh pits); many school situations (see didaskaleinophobia); Paris on July 14, 1789 (if you're a sufferer with access to a time machine).

||||| Phobia Trivia |||||

Crowds can in fact be very dangerous, as demonstrated in 1819 at the Peterloo Massacre in England when a gathering of 70,000 people went berserk after the military were sent in to break up the crowd. Fifteen people were crushed or trampled to death and many hundreds badly injured. So there is a genuine basis for this fear. Medical professionals advise against trying to help a sufferer by making them face their fears and exposing them to a large crowd. Enochlophobia is one of Woody Allen's many phobias.

||||| Statistics |||||

The largest crowd ever assembled was the Kumbh Mela pilgrimage in India in 2013, when 30 million people gathered. But perhaps more astonishing is the seventh largest crowd in history and the largest ever in the Western Hemisphere: a gathering of 5 million people in the streets of Chicago in 2016 when the Cubs won the World Series after a 108-year drought.

Entamaphobia

MEANING: fear of doors

ORIGIN: the Greek word *eisodos*, meaning "entrance"

ENTAMAPHOBIA is the fear of doors. Sufferers are afraid of all types of doors, open or closed. In addition to a fear of cramped spaces and suffocation, entamaphobia often features insecurity and fear of the unknown or what might be lurking on the other side of a door. Children can develop a fear of going through an open door, or associate closed doors with abandonment and solitude. Entamaphobes employ a number of methods to deal with their condition, going to great lengths to lock a door properly, installing several unnecessary locks, or tentatively peeking through an open door to check for dangers outside. Some get completely hysterical at the idea of walking through a door and avoid leaving the house, quit jobs, and refuse to undertake everyday errands like shopping for fear of encountering a dreaded door. This behavior can result in ridicule from family, friends, and colleagues, straining personal and professional relationships. With behavioral therapy and gradual desensitization, the patient is slowly exposed to both open and shut doors. Entamaphobes can take solace in the fact that they're not alone: Even the rock band The Killers, according to their song "Human," are potential sufferers, sometimes getting nervous when they see an open door.

THINGS TO AVOID: houses, buildings, and workplaces; cars and other vehicles and methods of transport; the band *The Doors*.

|||| Phobia Trivia ||||

Entamaphobia is often associated with claustrophobia (the fear of enclosed spaces). The actor Matthew McConaughey is a sufferer of the condition, specifically afraid of revolving doors.

|||| Statistics ||||

The average American home has 10 doors, while the White House has 412. That makes it unlikely that any entamaphobes will be running for office any time soon.

Ephebiphobia

MEANING: fear of teenagers

ORIGIN: the Greek word *ephebos*, meaning "youth" or "adolescent"

EPHEBIPHOBIA is the fear of teenagers and does not include younger children. The fear of teenagers is thought to exist throughout the Western world. People of older generations often see youths as lazy, ignorant, disengaged, threatening, impulsive, wild, and rude. Teens also tend to be more concerned with their peers than other people around them, increasing the segregation of youths from adults and adding to the estrangement between generations. All of these factors contribute to ephebiphobia. Some teenagers get involved with gangs that engage in violence and crime, which adds to the fear. Having a bad experience with a teenager can also lead to the condition. The ephebiphobe experiences extreme anxiety when faced with a teen, often feeling threatened, and will sometimes lash out or flee the scene, doing anything to avoid interacting with adolescents. Behavioral therapy is sometimes used to treat the condition; medications are rarely needed, except in the case of parents who have to live with moody teenagers on a daily basis. For them, self-medicating with alcoholic beverages often provides some relief and much-needed sanity.

THINGS TO AVOID: shopping malls; high schools; arcades and other teenage hangouts; Nickelodeon and Disney channels; Snapchat.

|||| Phobia Trivia ||||

Pedophobia is the fear of infants and children and is often incorrectly used for the fear of teenagers.

|||| Statistics ||||

In 2017 just under 810,000 arrests were made of people under the age of 18 in the U.S. That was 59 percent fewer than the number of arrests in 2008. So fear not, it is getting better for the ephebiphobes out there.

Ereuthrophobia

MEANING: fear of blushing

ORIGIN: the Greek word *erythros*, meaning "red"

Also spelled "erytophobia" or "erythrophobia," EREUTHRO-PHOBIA is the pathological fear of blushing. Blushing is an involuntary action, triggered by emotional stress or embarrassment. It is that feeling of embarrassment, as well as the inability to control blushing, that leads to ereuthrophobia. Sufferers often have low self-esteem and are petrified of the fact that blushing betrays their feelings, especially to people that they are attracted to. The blushing reaction itself is not the actual source of fear, but rather the attention that it draws and the emotions associated with it. Unfortunately, the fear of blushing often results in extreme anxiety and distress, which themselves can lead to blushing, creating a self-perpetuating problem. The most common treatment for ereuthrophobia is behavioral therapy, although in extreme cases surgery is performed to cut the sympathetic nerves responsible for blushing. Ereuthrophobes should, however, bear in mind that blushing is a natural phenomenon and nothing to be afraid of. That said, in his 1872 book *The Expression of the Emotions in Man and Animals*, the great English naturalist Charles Darwin described blushing as "the most peculiar and most human of all expressions," so perhaps there is a little more to this common reaction than people realize at first blush.

THINGS TO AVOID: public embarrassment; compliments from someone you are attracted to; makeup stores.

The face turns red when you blush because facial skin has more capillary loops and a higher density of blood vessels than other skin areas. These blood vessels are also wider in diameter, are nearer to the surface, and their visibility is less diminished by tissue fluid. Some suggest that blushing is the result of our instinctual fight-or-flight mechanism when physical action is not possible or realistic. Sufferers of ereuthrophobia also sometimes suffer from hemophobia (the fear of blood), because red is the color of blood. Despite having a close physiological relation, blushing is distinguished from flushing, which is more intensive, extends over more of the body, and doesn't generally have an emotional source.

||||| Statistics |||||

While a blush can occur within a few seconds of an embarrassing event, it generally takes between one and two minutes to disappear—an eternity for the average ereuthrophobe.

Ergophobia

MEANING: fear of work

ORIGIN: the Greek word *ergon*, meaning "work"

Also known as ergasiophobia, ERGOPHOBIA is the persistent fear of work and searching for employment, and can affect both those who have held jobs before and those who have never worked. This complex phobia may actually be a combination of fears, such as fear of failure, fear of responsibility, fear of speaking in front of groups, and fear of socializing.

The sufferer may also be afraid of performing manual labor for fear of getting injured, although most ergophobic individuals are also afraid of any kind of labor. Sufferers have often had a work-related trauma, such as workplace bullying or harassment, or a boss who demanded too much (like Miranda Priestly from *The Devil Wears Prada*). Getting humiliated at work or fired from a job can also trigger the phobia, as can the anxiety of job hunting and the fear of rejection. While most people have a natural and understandable aversion to getting up and going to work daily, the ergophobe actually fears it. Symptoms include nausea, a foggy feeling, desire to run away or hide, crying, panic attacks, and thoughts of dying. Victims of this debilitating condition often don't show up for work, and sometimes turn to alcohol or drug abuse. This can lead to demotion or termination from work, adding to the fear. Since work is necessary to survival for most people, treatment of ergophobia is essential. In addition to behavioral and cognitive therapy, gradual desensitization, where the patient is given small tasks to do before building up to larger tasks, has had some success. Those friends of yours who don't work? Perhaps they're not completely lazy after all—maybe they actually have ergophobia. Or maybe, like many of us, they just don't like work.

THINGS TO AVOID: the workforce; looking for work; thinking about or watching work; the Rihanna song "Work" featuring Drake; the Roy Orbison song "Working for the Man"; the Dolly Parton song "9 to 5."

|||| Phobia Trivia ||||

In Roman times before the advent of canned goods and refrigeration, salt was a valuable commodity and soldiers received some of their wages in salt. This was known as a "salarium," from the word *sal*, for "salt." That is where the modern word "salary" comes from.

It is estimated that the average American spends around 90,000 hours of their lives at work. That's a lot of time for the ergophobe to avoid. In years, it amounts to a little over 10— maybe it doesn't sound quite as daunting that way.

Euphobia

MEANING: fear of good news

ORIGIN: the Greek word *eu*, meaning "good"

EUPHOBIA is the irrational fear of good news, specifically hearing or receiving good news. Most people always want to hear the good news, and fear the bad news, but some fear only the good news and thrive in the negative. These euphobes are not so much afraid of hearing the good news, but what might ensue, as they tend to believe that good news is always followed by bad. This phobia is usually caused by past experiences of disappointment after good news: for example, hearing that you've won the lottery, only to find out that you had the right numbers but the wrong date. The typical euphobe thrives in a chaotic environment and displays symptoms of anxiety and panic upon hearing good news, which they equate with confusion and a lack of control. They may also limit themselves to a group of friends who share a negative outlook. Treatment includes behavioral psychotherapy to help the patient learn how to feel happy, rather than anxious, upon hearing good news, and to learn the correct answer to the age-old question: "Do you want the good news or the bad news first?"

THINGS TO AVOID: glass-half-full types; the *Good News Bible*.

The word euphoria has similar origins: *Eu* means "good" and *pherein* means "to bear."

The *Good News Bible* has sold over 150 million copies worldwide.

Eurotophobia

MEANING: fear of female genitals

ORIGIN: unknown, although the Greek word *eurotas* means "a river"

EUROTOPHOBIA is the persistent fear of female genitals, often originating from a prudish and puritanical upbringing. An extreme aversion to perceived by-products of the female genitalia, such as discharge, mucus, or odor, can also trigger eurotophobia. The condition can manifest itself in both men and women; for men, often because of an unfamiliarity and lack of understanding of the female genitalia and, for women, sometimes because of the threat of genital mutilation or female circumcision, particularly in some African countries. Some medical students, particularly those in obstetrics, have also been known to develop this phobia, at times leading them to drop out of school. Many eurotophobes will do anything they can to avoid having sex and will refuse to even look at a naked woman, and female sufferers refuse to look at themselves. This can result in introversion, relationship difficulties, and the compulsion to use euphemisms when referring to the female genitalia. If an audacious sufferer does decide to attempt copulation, illuminated venues will generally be avoided, and if a daytime foray is attempted, bed sheets will usually be employed to hide what terrifies the eurotophobe. Should these safety measures fail, however, the eurotophobe is likely to sweat profusely, tremble, vomit, cry hysterically, and flee, none of which is generally considered conducive to romance.

THINGS TO AVOID: unclothed women; sex; pornography.

||||| Phobia Trivia |||||

Eurotophobia is related to kolpophobia; however, the latter is broader, allowing for the inclusion of all sex organs.

||||| Statistics |||||

According to the World Health Organization, it is estimated that more than 200 million women alive today have undergone female genital mutilation in over 30 countries, particularly in Africa, the Middle East, and Asia.

Is for Frigophobia

Flatulophobia

MEANING: fear of farting

ORIGIN: the Latin word *flatus*, meaning "blowing"

Also spelled "flatuphobia," FLATULOPHOBIA is the fear of farting, and generally includes one's own farts as well as the farts of others. Generally caused by the smells and sounds associated with farting, a past  fart-related incident—like passing audible wind in a public setting or a mishap involving a fart gone wrong that resulted in soiling—can lead to the phobia. Sufferers of this condition are prone to anxiety in the presence of farting; smelling or hearing a fart often causes them to panic and flee the fart-ridden scene. Mild flatulophobes stay away from people known to be habitual public farters, while severe sufferers avoid all social settings, often becoming reclusive and only contacting people in the written form (since even phone contact contains the risk of hearing a particularly loud fart). Flatulophobia is generally treated with hypnotherapy and flatulence education. Exposure therapy is also used, the patient presumably forced to endure an array of farts until farting is no longer a source of consternation and panic. People in the advanced stages of flatulophobia will not even break wind alone in private places. While holding in a fart is unlikely to cause any long-term physical damage, it can result in constipation and pain, so it is recommended that flatulophobes face their fears, and let it all out. If the thought of that is too much to bear, you could try burping out any excess wind instead—that is, unless you suffer from eructophobia, the fear of burping, as well.

THINGS TO AVOID: eating anything, but particularly beans; being around others who eat; drinking gaseous drinks; Whoopee cushions; toilet humor.

For centuries it has been believed that retaining flatulence could be dangerous. The Roman Emperor Claudius even passed a law legalizing farting at banquets because of the health concerns involved. Flatulence is a mixture of gases that are produced by bacteria and yeast in the intestinal tract. The gases primarily consist of oxygen, nitrogen, carbon dioxide, hydrogen, and methane. The presence of sulfuric components is responsible for the common odor. These gases are not poisonous, although retaining them can result in a distension of the bowel, potentially leading to constipation, bloating, abdominal pain, and even bad breath.

Most animals and all mammals fart. The average person releases up to 1.5 liters of gas per day.

Frigophobia

MEANING: fear of cold

ORIGIN: the Latin word *frigo*, meaning "cold"

Also known as cheimaphobia, cheimatophobia, and psychro-phobia, FRIGOPHOBIA is the extreme fear of cold or cold things. While many people enjoy cold weather and cannot tolerate heat and humidity, frigophobes loathe the cold and are actually fearful of it. This phobia has some legitimate basis, as extreme cold can cause hypothermia and frostbite. Sufferers have often had a negative experience with the cold, like being trapped in cold conditions, falling into a freezing lake, or getting stuck in the snow. It can also be related to cold weather's association with loneliness and staying home, or something as trivial as eating ice cream and getting brain freeze. Frigophobes prefer to live in tropical climates, and avoid air-conditioned places and winter pastimes like skiing. They keep their homes very warm and bundle up in heavy clothes and blankets, regardless of air temperature or time of the year. The onset of winter can cause the frigophobe to have heart palpitations, shortness of breath, and, of course, uncontrollable shivering from both cold and fear. Extreme sufferers even refuse cold desserts and ice in their drinks. Medications are rarely needed to treat this condition; psychotherapy and education about the cold are the best approaches. And if you're a frigophobe and still love the taste of ice cream, all hope is not lost. Just wait a few minutes between brain freezes—it's worth it.

THINGS TO AVOID: Alaska; Canada; Russia; the North Pole; winter; ice; refrigerators, particularly the freezer compartment; snow; perhaps ice cream.

|||| Phobia Trivia ||||

There are a number of phobias closely related to frigophobia. Cryophobia (the fear of extreme cold) is considered a branch of frigophobia, while pagophobia (the fear of ice or frost) is a separate phobia. In China, it is thought by some that frigophobia may be linked to *koro*, a disorder that causes male sufferers to feel like his penis is retracting into the body (also known as "genital retraction syndrome," or "shrinking penis"). Believed to be caused by an insufficiency of the male element *yang*, sufferers correlate coldness with an overabundance of the female element *yin*. To rebalance the *yin* and *yang* and rectify this condition, sufferers are put on a strict diet that includes ground ginger, turnip juice mixed with ginger and honey, red tea with ginger and sugar, various spices (including chili pepper and more ginger), vinegar diluted in water, and chicken soup.

||||| Statistics |||||

The coldest place on Earth is in Antarctica, where the lowest temperature ever recorded was -133.6°F. The coldest temperature recorded in the contiguous U.S. was -70°F in Rogers Pass, Montana, in 1954.

Is for Globophobia

Gallophobia

MEANING: fear of the French

ORIGIN: the Latin word *Gallicus*, meaning "Gaul"

Sometimes spelled "galiophobia" and also known as francophobia, GALLOPHOBIA is the fear or intense hatred of France, French people, and French culture. Surprisingly common, although often unexpressed, it can extend to the French government and any population who speaks French, such as French Guiana in South America. America has a long history of friendship with France. French nobles volunteered as officers in the American Revolutionary War, which the French government helped to fund. In the late 1800s, the Statue of Liberty was gifted to America by the people of France. France allied  with the United States during the first Gulf War and French forces have played a role in the War in Afghanistan since 2001. So where does gallophobia originate? There was some American anti-French sentiment in the wake of France's 2003 refusal to support U.S. military action against Iraq. This may have inspired more recent gallophobes, causing them to avoid or openly hate anything to do with the French. More enduring sufferers, however, sometimes cite historic French colonization, their perceived higher standards of living, and the fact that the French appear arrogant. But given what France and its culture has to offer (see Things to Avoid), gallophobia seems like a self-imposed condition that comes with a lot of costs.

THINGS TO AVOID: frog's legs; snails (in the edible form); long, phallic loaves of white bread; a lot of good cheeses, wine, and champagne; French restaurants and cuisine; statuettes of the Eiffel Tower; berets; saying "oui oui."

There have been a number of prominent examples of gallophobia in recent times: the derogatory phrase "cheese-eating surrender monkeys" began as a joke on *The Simpsons* in 1995, suggesting that the French are cowards. In this century, bumper stickers and T-shirts called for the U.S. to invade "Iraq first, France next" and "First Iraq, then Chirac!"

It is estimated that during the French Revolution, at least 40,000 people were killed and 300,000 people were arrested.

Geliophobia

MEANING: fear of laughter

ORIGIN: the Greek word *gelo*, meaning "laugh"

Also spelled "gelophobia," GELIOPHOBIA is the abnormal fear of laughter or laughing (and not the fear of Jell-O, despite what the name suggests). It is usually caused by a bad experience, like embarrassment about having laughed inappropriately or being laughed at as a child. People who suffer from this phobia are subjected to emotional turmoil that is disruptive to their ability to function. They find jokes, comedic performances, funny situations, and funny people to be sources of extreme anxiety, and experience trembling, numbness, and even paralysis at the slightest suggestion of humor. The vast majority of cases are self-diagnosed, making statistical records difficult to compile. Humorless talk therapy and self-help techniques have been known to diminish the condition, but medication is rarely needed (in this case, laughter is NOT the best medicine). Indeed, geliophobia is no laughing matter.

THINGS TO AVOID: comedy clubs; comedy films and TV shows with laugh tracks; frivolity, shenanigans, ballyhoo, and tomfoolery; the first Sunday of May, which is internationally recognized World Laughter Day.

Phobia Trivia

Although they can potentially overlap, this phobia should not be confused with gelotophobia, which is the fear of being laughed at. Kim Kardashian, who is a sufferer of rhytiphobia (fear of wrinkles), openly admits that she rarely laughs for fear of aging. This does not necessarily make her a geliophobe as well, but it does make her a rather dire dinner companion.

Statistics

An Ethiopian man named Belachew Girma holds the unofficial record for the longest bout of laughter. At an event in 2010, he laughed incessantly for three hours and six minutes. Unfortunately for Mr. Girma, there was no Guinness World Record official present to verify the record. Clearly not a sufferer of geliophobia, Mr. Girma heads a nonprofit organization called Laughter for All Ethiopia.

Genuphobia

MEANING: fear of knees

ORIGIN: the Latin word *genu*, meaning "knee"

Sometimes caused by an injury to the knee, GENUPHOBIA is the fear of knees, including one's own knees, someone else's knees, or, in many cases, the act of kneeling. Genuphobes find knees extraordinarily ugly and are scared of looking at them, sometimes out of unfamiliarity because of having grown up in an environment where people exclusively wore long pants. Others fear knees and kneeling because of an association with submissiveness and servility. Sufferers of genuphobia keep their knees covered, avoiding activities like swimming and other sports, as well as jobs that involve kneeling. Some avoid crossing their legs because of the emphasis it places on the knees. Even the sight of bare knees on television can result in extreme anxiety, shortness of breath, and dizziness. Treatment includes behavioral therapy and medication, but, whatever you do, don't get down on your knees and pray for help.

THINGS TO AVOID: summer; beaches and swimming pools and other places where knees are likely to be on display; pre-schools and kindergarten where the song "Head, Shoulders, Knees, and Toes" is a crowd favorite; churches and other places of prayer; the Guns N' Roses song "Welcome to the Jungle."

Phobia Trivia

The human knee is a compound, modified hinge joint, and is the largest joint in the human body. At birth, the kneecap is made of cartilage, which ossifies to bone between the ages of three and five years. The elephant is the only animal that has four forward-facing knees.

Between 1999 and 2008, U.S. emergency rooms saw over 6.6 million knee injuries. That is a rate of 2.29 knee injuries per 1,000 people. People between 15 and 24 years old had the highest knee injury rate, while children younger than five had the lowest.

Gephyrophobia

MEANING: fear of bridges

ORIGIN: the Greek word *gephura*, meaning "bridge"

Also spelled "gephydrophobia" or "gephysrophobia," GEPHYROPHOBIA is the extreme fear of bridges, particularly of crossing bridges. The phobia may arise from fear of driving off a bridge, wind blowing one off a bridge, or that a bridge will collapse. Gephyrophobia often overlaps with acrophobia (the fear of heights); however, it can also exist with small and restrictive bridges, sometimes accompanied by claustrophobia, or the fear of enclosed spaces. Witnessing an accident or a death on a bridge, or watching movie scenes or news reports depicting tragic bridge-related events, can also lead to gephyrophobia. Symptoms include light-headedness, dizziness, and a feeling of being trapped; sufferers of this condition limit the area in which they travel and may drive miles out of their way to avoid bridges. Gephyrophobia affects both one's professional and personal lives, and can endanger actual lives if the extreme gephyrophobe were to swerve or brake suddenly when confronted with a bridge.

THINGS TO AVOID: Venice and Amsterdam; San Francisco; "The Bridge" episode of *The Middle*, where Brick is plagued by the phobia; the video game *Halo: Combat Evolved*, which includes a map called gephryophobia (likely named because many players are killed on the bridge); *The Bridges of Madison County* (book and film); the scene in *Harry Potter and the Half-Blood Prince* where Death Eaters attack the Millennium Bridge.

|||| Phobia Trivia ||||

A number of U.S. authorities offer special assistance for motorists who need help crossing certain bridges, and in some cases will arrange for someone else to drive the car over the bridge—examples include the Mackinac Bridge in Michigan, the San Francisco–Oakland Bay Bridge, and the Chesapeake Bay Bridge in Maryland.

|||| Statistics ||||

The longest bridge in the world is the Danyang–Kunshan Grand Bridge in China, which is 102.4 miles long. The tallest bridge in the world is the Millau Viaduct in southern France. Its highest point is 1,104 feet, which is 41 feet taller than the Eiffel Tower!

Gerontophobia

MEANING: fear of old people

ORIGIN: the Greek word *geron*, meaning "old man"

GERONTOPHOBIA is the intense fear of old people. This phobia is borne out of a lack of understanding about old people or anxiety about death and people who appear extremely frail. Geronto-phobia can also be caused by an unsavory interaction with an old person. The fact that some old people are forgetful, smell weird, can't hear very well, and are grumpy can also incite geronto-phobia. Sufferers experience rapid breathing, heart palpitations, thoughts of dying, and a detachment from reality in the presence of old people. Breathing techniques are often used to handle stressful encounters with old people; systematic desensitization is also commonly used to treat the condition. Education on the ways of the elderly can also help sufferers transition from fear to understanding. But whether you fear old people or not, you shouldn't judge old men for being grumpy: Science says it's not their fault (see Phobia Trivia below).

THINGS TO AVOID: retirement and nursing homes; Florida; the 46 million Americans who are over 65; Neil Young's song "Old Man"; John Fogerty's song "The Old Man Down the Road."

|||| Phobia Trivia ||||

Gerontophobia is closely related to gerascophobia, which is the fear of getting old. Also known as "grumpy old man complex" or "irritable male syndrome," crankiness in older men is the result of several factors. In addition to emotional changes and feelings of worthlessness, changes in the brain are at the root of the condition. As men age, testosterone levels fall, leading to fatigue, depression, and a reduction in libido and concentration. This often leads to irritability. There is, however, another key change that takes place: Men lose brain tissue in the frontal lobe at almost three times the rate of women. The frontal lobe is involved in motor function, memory, problem solving, concentration, reasoning, and impulse control. The result of the decline? A grumpy old man.

Statistics

According to the National Center for Health Statistics, the average American lifespan in 1960 was 67, while in 2016 it was almost 79. So things are only getting scarier for the geronto-phobes out there.

Globophobia

MEANING: fear of balloons

ORIGIN: the Greek word *globo*, meaning "sphere"

GLOBOPHOBIA is the irrational fear of balloons. Normally associated with fun and festivity, balloons are anything but for the globophobe, who goes to extreme lengths to avoid birthday parties, circuses, and anything that might involve the colorful, air-filled decorations. Globophobes refuse to touch or get within close proximity to a balloon for fear it will pop, making a sudden explosive sound. They also fear the sight, smell, and squeaky sound made by a balloon being twisted into the shape of a cute dog or swan. In extreme cases, just the thought of a balloon can send the sufferer into a blind panic. Interestingly, most globophobes can tolerate deflated balloons. While the phobia is more common in young children, it can continue into adulthood and is usually caused by a negative balloon-related experience, such as having one explode in the face. Being teased or bullied about the condition exacerbates it. In the heightened emotional state of a birthday party, an unexpected balloon popping can be disastrous for the globophobe. What's more, globophobes also often distrust anyone holding a balloon, such as a clown, which can be a catalyst for coulrophobia (the fear of clowns). Hypnotherapy has been known to have some success in bursting the fear—oh no, it's back!

THINGS TO AVOID: birthday parties; circuses; parades; weddings; fairgrounds; political rallies; Fourth of July celebrations; clowns; hot air balloons; water balloons.

|||| Phobia Trivia ||||

While it is a very uncommon phobia, Oprah Winfrey is a self-confessed globophobe, likening the popping sound to gunfire and saying that, "It just really freaks me out being around balloons." Stand-up comedian Doug Stanhope is also a sufferer, as is South Korean actor So Ji-sub.

|||| Statistics ||||

It is estimated that between 45 and 50 million balloons are sold in California alone each year—perhaps not the best place for globophobes to live.

Gynophobia

MEANING: fear of women

ORIGIN: the Greek word *gune*, meaning "woman"

Also known as gynephobia or feminophobia, GYNOPHOBIA is the abnormal fear of women and is typically suffered by men. Gynophobia stems from feelings of ill will toward mothers and sisters, sometimes extending to all women and resulting in misogyny. Gynophobes often fear having sex with women and avoid marriage as a result, sometimes turning to homosexuality (at least that was the prevailing theory in the late 1800s). Psychologists attribute this phobia to unresolved maternal conflicts, childhood abandonment, or mental or physical abuse by mothers. When the symptoms continue into adulthood, women are seen as a physical or emotional threat, resulting in a mistrust of all women. The genesis of this mistrust may also be a rejection or humiliation at the hands of a woman. It is even believed that stories about witches can trigger the phobia, although the more specific wiccaphobia (which is not a fear of Wikipedia, unless you're reading the page about witches) addresses that fear. Gynophobia can have wide-ranging implications for the sufferer, including inability to form relationships with women or even work with them, especially women in positions of power. Symptoms vary for gynophobes, but might include shortness of breath, rapid heart rate, inability to form words and sentences, and headaches. Talk therapy (presumably with a male counselor) has had some success in treating gynophobia.

THINGS TO AVOID: women; witches; hospital maternity wards and any other place likely to have a preponderance of women.

There is also a phobia for the abnormal or irrational fear of men—androphobia. Related to gynophobia is venustaphobia or caligynephobia, which is the fear of beautiful women (a condition not suffered by Hugh Hefner). This condition, however, arises for vastly different reasons and affects most men, although the symptoms are often the same: shortness of breath, rapid heart rate, and inability to form words and sentences.

||||| Statistics |||||

Females comprise almost 51 percent of the population of the U.S. While that might not seem a great disparity, it does amount to an extra 3.3 million women for gynophobes to avoid. Scary enough.

Is for
Haphephobia

Halitophobia

MEANING: fear of bad breath

ORIGIN: the Latin word *halitus*, meaning "breath"

HALITOPHOBIA is the fear of bad breath—or halitosis—either one's own or the breath of others, often caused by the trauma of being forced to smell someone's rancid breath. In relation to one's own breath, this phobia is often borne out of the pursuit of perfection and fear at the thought of someone else finding you repulsive. In any case, the condition leads to isolation and avoiding socialization. Halitophobes prefer speaking on the phone wherever possible and, in the presence of other people, sit as far away as possible. This can make social gatherings awkward and romantic relationships really, really weird. Sufferers who fear their own bad breath use mouthwash excessively and regularly check their own breath. This can lead to depression and obsessive-compulsive disorder. When the average halitophobe comes into contact with bad breath, they experience nausea, sweating, panic, and desperation to flee the offending breath, which can be particularly difficult when they themselves are the culprit. Halitophobia is typically (and cruelly) treated by exposure therapy, a risky technique that could result in compounding the condition or making the sufferer pass out.

THINGS TO AVOID: garlic; onions; forgetting to brush or floss; getting too close to other people; kissing, especially if you are also a philemaphobe (afraid of kissing).

Halitophobia is a branch of both osmophobia (the fear of odors) and bromidrophobia (the fear of body odors). Garlic is the worst food for bad breath because it contains a sulfuric compound called allyl methyl sulfide (AMS). AMS promotes the growth of microbes in the mouth that cause bad breath, exacerbating the problem. AMS is also a gas that is absorbed into the blood during the metabolism of garlic. From the blood it is transferred to the lungs where it is then exhaled as garlic breath. Because the garlic is in your bloodstream and is exhaled in your breath, there is very little you can do to get rid of it except wait until it has passed through your body. Thorough brushing will only do so much, although consuming parsley, lemon, tea, or milk are thought to help.

||||| Statistics |||||

Halitophobia is thought to affect about 1 percent of Americans. Research also suggests that 98 percent of people have had bad breath at some point.

Haphephobia

MEANING: fear of being touched

ORIGIN: the ancient Greek word *haphe*, meaning "touch"

HAPHEPHOBIA is the extreme fear of being touched. It is usually caused by an acute exaggeration of normal tendencies to protect one's personal space, and affects people with highly anxious dispositions. Sufferers see touching as an invasion of personal space and fear contamination from physical contact, even from people they know and trust. While haphephobia is innate in some people, others develop it as the result of a bad experience like an assault, and it can manifest as a fear of being touched by men only. Sufferers avoid crowds and other places where they are likely to be touched and, in extreme cases, avoid people altogether and become reclusive. The phobia has an adverse effect on the sufferer's personal life and relationships when the slightest touch results in extreme anxiety and panic. Sex, for the haphephobe, is an implausible concept, making this a particularly unfortunate phobia to deal with.

THINGS TO AVOID: crowds; people; romantic relationships; the 1962 movie *David and Lisa* where David is committed to a mental hospital for haphephobia.

Phobia Trivia

Haphephobia is also known as aphephobia, aphenphosmphobia, haphophobia, hapnophobia, haptephobia, haptophobia, and thixophobia.

Statistics

Different cultures treat touching differently. South American, Middle Eastern, and Mediterranean countries are considered "contact cultures" by many, while Asia, North America, and Northern Europe are largely "noncontact cultures."

Hedonophobia

MEANING: fear of feeling pleasure

ORIGIN: the Greek word *hedon*, meaning "pleasure"

HEDONOPHOBIA is the fear of feeling pleasure, including love, joy, happiness, or pride. Also called hedenophobia, this fear is often linked to sexual intercourse and apprehension over losing control. It can stem from being told as a child that sex is dirty and wrong. Guilt over engaging in joyful activities while others experience pain or hardship can bring on the phobia, especially in cultural and religious settings that consider pleasurable pursuits frivolous and inappropriate. Indeed, an acetic upbringing can result in hedonophobia (or, conversely, rebellion). Other sufferers feel undeserving of pleasure, that they aren't entitled to feel good, or that things are too good to be true. Hedonophobes avoid intimate relationships, sex, drinking, sporting events, gourmet food, television and films, and other activities deemed to be pleasurable or joyful in any way. Unsurprisingly, this condition is quite rare.

THINGS TO AVOID: intimacy and sex; vacations; alcohol; drugs; food; having any fun whatsoever.

‖‖‖ Phobia Trivia ‖‖‖

Hedonism is the pursuit of pleasure as the primary priority in life. Various forms of hedonism have been practiced in most cultures since the times of the ancient Egyptians and the ancient Greeks, who certainly knew how to have fun (outside of all the monument building and slavery, that is).

‖‖‖ Statistics ‖‖‖

In a 2018 study on American guilty pleasures by Vudu.com, ordering takeout topped the list (42 percent of people included it in their top 30), followed by falling asleep in front of the TV, which 41 percent of people included.

Heliophobia

MEANING: fear of the sun

ORIGIN: the Greek word *helios*, meaning "sun"

HELIOPHOBIA is the fear of the sun, sunlight, or any bright light. Sometimes caused by a severe sunburn or an experience with skin cancer, heliophobia is usually a type of health anxiety; sufferers believe that avoiding the sun will prevent skin cancer. For those with body image issues, it can arise from a concern with the premature aging effects of the sun. Other medical conditions, such as keratoconus (an eye disorder resulting in optic sensitivity to sunlight) or migraines triggered by bright light, can also trigger the phobia. Heliophobes tend to cover themselves with long, protective clothing or carry an umbrella when venturing outdoors during the daytime. More extreme sufferers refuse to go outside when the sun is out. This can lead to a vitamin D deficiency, as well as depression and feelings of alienation. When encountering sunlight, heliophobes experience parched mouth, sweating, muscle cramps, heightened senses, and a desperate desire to flee, which is not easy, since the sun covers approximately half the Earth at any given time. What's worse is that avoiding the sun altogether can lead people to suspect you're a vampire. This could lead to them developing sanguivoriphobia (the fear of vampires), a far scarier condition than heliophobia.

THINGS TO AVOID: daylight; people named Ray; California; Australia; The Beatles song "Here Comes the Sun"; the song

"Heliophobe" by German rock band Scumbucket; the film *The Benchwarmers*; the Bruce Springsteen song "Waitin' on a Sunny Day"; the Ray Charles song "That Lucky Old Sun."

|||| Phobia Trivia ||||

A fear of the sun is a branch of astrophobia (the fear of celestial objects), and a fear of sunlight is a branch of photophobia (the fear of light). Sometimes called the vampire phobia, heliophobia is considered by some to be a telltale sign of a vampire. A fear of sunshine is one of Woody Allen's many phobias, so perhaps he's a vampire after all.

|||| Statistics ||||

The sun is 93 million miles from Earth, 4.5 billion years old, and could fit over 1 million Earths inside of it. It takes 8 minutes and 20 seconds for light from the sun to reach Earth.

Hexakosioihexekontahexaphobia

MEANING: fear of the number 666

ORIGIN: the Greek words *hexakosioi*, meaning "six hundred," *hexekonta*, meaning "sixty," and *hex*, meaning "six"

HEXAKOSIOIHEXEKONTAHEXAPHOBIA is the extreme fear of the number 666, the "Number of the Beast." The number 666 has long been considered evil—the devil's number. This stems from the Bible. In the Book of Revelation in the New Testament (13:15–18), 666 is associated with the Beast of Revelation, one of two mythological creatures described in the book (one comes out of the sea, the other out of the Earth). The number is widely recognized as the mark of the

Antichrist, or the devil, and has been used in popular culture as a reference to the devil. This widespread use can lead to hexakosioihexekontahexaphobia, causing sufferers extreme anxiety when they see or think about the number. Some hexakosioihexekontahexaphobes draw connections between unrelated events, especially if something bad happens soon after their exposure to the number. They refuse to live in a home with 666 as part of the address, and avoid the number in their daily lives: blocking channel 666 from cable listings, driving farther to change an odometer from 666 to 667, or buying extra groceries to avoid a total of $66.60.

THINGS TO AVOID: the number 6 (if you have blurred vision); the films *The Omen* (original and remake), *The Doom Generation*, *Pulp Fiction*, *Bedazzled*, *End of Days*, and *The Phantom of the Opera*; Iron Maiden's song "The Number of the Beast"; Satanic meetings and rituals.

|||| Phobia Trivia ||||

Many people avoid things related to 666, like Ronald and Nancy Reagan, who were potential hexakosioihexekontahexaphobes. In 1989, when they moved from the White House to their home in Bel Air, Los Angeles, they had its address changed from 666 St. Cloud Road to 668 St. Cloud Road. U.S. Highway 666, known as the "Devil's Highway," had a high rate of fatalities along its New Mexico section, some say because of its number. The route's name was changed to U.S. Highway 491 in 2003.

|||| Statistics ||||

666 is the sum of the numbers 1 through 36, which are also the numbers on a roulette wheel. It is also the sum of the squares of the first seven prime numbers.

Hippopotomonstrosesquippedaliophobia

MEANING: fear of long words

ORIGIN: a combination of the Greek words *hippo* and *potam-os*, meaning "river horse" or something very large, and the Latin words *monstrum*, meaning "monstrous being," and *sesquippedali*, meaning "measuring a foot and a half long"

HIPPOPOTOMONSTROSESQUIPPEDALIOPHOBIA is often considered a fictional phobia, but the fear of long words is actually very real. While many people are amused or intrigued by long and unusual words, sufferers of this phobia experience a great deal of anxiety when faced with linguistic behemoths. It is believed that this phobia is not inherent in people, but is caused by a traumatic experience involving lengthy words. A child at school may have been laughed at for mispronouncing a long word, resulting in stammering, shaking, or discombobulation (exacerbated if someone were to utter the word "discombobulation"). The unsavory incident is stored in the recesses of the brain, and seeing a long word at a later time results in feelings of dread and terror, eliciting the same physical response. Even with an understanding that the fear is irrational, the abnormal reaction cannot be controlled, although self-help techniques like deep breathing and relaxation have been known to lessen the symptoms. Gradual exposure to long words has also produced positive results. It is, however, both ironic and unfortunate for hippopotomonstrosesquippedaliophobes that the 14-syllable term for the phobia is itself one of the longest words in the English language.

THINGS TO AVOID: mortgage applications and fine print of any sort; dictionaries; lawyers and professors; the actual term for the phobia.

Sesquipedalophobia was the original term for the phobia, but "hippopotomonstro" was added as a prefix to augment the intensity of the word and to make it even longer and more tormenting to its sufferers. Hippopotomonstroses-quippedaliophobia is considered one of the weirdest and most unusual phobias in existence, but Canadian YouTube personality Matthew Santoro is a longtime sufferer.

|||| Statistics ||||

The longest English word comprises 45 letters. It is pneu-monoultramicroscopicsilicovolcanoconiosis, which is a lung disease.

Hodophobia

MEANING: fear of travel

ORIGIN: the Latin word *hodo*, meaning "traveling" or "road"

HODOPHOBIA is the intense fear of travel. While many people experience anxiety at the inconvenience and expense of travel, hodophobes are actually afraid of it. Hodophobia is the generalized fear of all types of travel, distinct from the fear of specific methods of transportation, like planes or trains. The condition is rooted in the unpleasant feeling of being in an unfamiliar place or away from home. It manifests in an inability to leave home and shaking, sweating, crying, and gastrointestinal distress at the prospect of travel. When travel is necessary, the hodophobe finds difficulty in navigation, packing, following security procedures, and dealing with delays. Minor things, like deciding where to eat while away from home, can cause extreme anxiety and confusion. Even traveling to a place of work can become an impossibility for some, impacting the sufferer's livelihood and social life. Early planning and organization are the best-known techniques for reducing travel anxiety; traveling with a partner and visualizing the journey ahead of time can also help mitigate dread.

THINGS TO AVOID: Jack Kerouac; planes, trains, and automobiles (and the movie by that title); roads; airports; travel agencies; *The Amazing Race;* many television commercials.

Phobia Trivia

Sigmund Freud confessed in a number of letters to a fear of travel, using the German term *Reiseangst,* meaning "travel anxiety." Hodophobia is related to siderodromophobia, which is the fear of trains, railroads, and traveling on trains.

Statistics

The farthest city to travel to from New York City is Perth, Australia, at 11,613 miles away. Best to avoid Perth altogether if you're a hodophobe: Perth is actually the farthest city from 179 other destinations.

Is for Iatrophobia

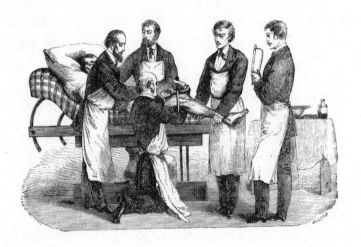

Iatrophobia

MEANING: fear of doctors

ORIGIN: the Greek word *iatros*, meaning "healer"

Sometimes known as "white coat hypertension," IATRO-PHOBIA, the fear of doctors, is common in young children, although many adults suffer from it as well. Iatrophobes put off a doctor's visit no matter how urgently they need it, preferring to suffer the pain rather than the anxiety of medical attention. Iatrophobia often begins with a traumatic childhood incident that required medical attention, or it can arise from the association of doctors with illness and death. Medical films, news reports, and statistics about medical malpractice can contribute to skepticism, if not outright fear, of doctors. Doctors are seen as authority figures by many people, creating a problem for those with difficulty following authority. Symptoms include nausea, elevated blood pressure, and gastrointestinal maladies. It can even lead to hypochondria, an obsessive worry about becoming ill. The phobia can become life-threatening if the sufferer refuses important vaccinations (common for those who also suffer from aichmophobia, a fear of needles or pointed objects) or other needed medical interventions. Treating the condition is difficult: The iatrophobe unlikely to seek help from a doctor.

THINGS TO AVOID: hospitals; *Botched*; *ER*; *Grey's Anatomy*; *General Hospital*.

||||| Phobia Trivia |||||

Iatrophobia often occurs side by side with dentophobia, which is the somewhat less-dangerous fear of dentists.

It is believed that many people die each year because of their refusal to seek medical help. That said, there is some serious justification for the fear of doctors: After heart disease and cancer, medical mistakes are the third leading cause of death in the U.S. According to a 2018 study by Johns Hopkins, over 250,000 Americans die from medical mistakes each year.

Ichthyophobia

MEANING: fear of fish

ORIGIN: the Greek word *ichthus*, meaning "fish"

ICHTHYOPHOBIA is the fear of fish. It ranges from the fear of eating fish to the fear of touching fish and the fear of dead fish. It can be triggered by a negative interaction, like getting bitten or startled by a fish. Being the target of a cruel prank, like a chopped fish head placed on your pillow, can also cause the phobia. The fact that fish are slimy, smelly creatures can lead to ichthyophobia, as can a belief that fish are responsible for illnesses and contain contaminants that can lead to mercury poisoning. While it is common and reasonable to fear sharks, ichthyophobes are afraid of even small and harmless fish. The sight or smell of a fish, dead or alive, causes either paralysis or a need to flee. Some ichthyophobes won't even go to the beach or cross bridges over water, while others refuse to go near aquariums. In severe cases, individuals will even refuse to visit the homes of friends with pet fish. Fish education is the most common form of treatment. The traumatic technique of radical exposure therapy, or "flooding," involves immersing the sufferer in a tank full of fish and can have positive results— just make sure to use goldfish and not piranhas.

THINGS TO AVOID: aquariums; fish tanks; oceans; rivers; dams; lakes; seafood restaurants; grocery stores; fishmongers; the film *Finding Nemo*.

| | | | Phobia Trivia | | | |

Ichthyophobia is related to ostraconophobia (the fear of shellfish), selachophobia or galeophobia (the fear of sharks), and enydreiophobia (the fear of fish tanks). The Navajo tribes fear all kinds of aquatic animals, but their fear is cultural rather than psychological. They believe that all aquatic beings are taboo and so refuse to touch or eat them, or even dive into waters where they might be present for fear of encountering them.

| | | | Statistics | | | |

There are over 33,600 known species of fish, the majority of which live in the Pacific Ocean. There are at least 1,200 species of venomous fish that all people—not just ichthyophobes— should avoid.

Ithyphallophobia

MEANING: fear of an erect penis

ORIGIN: the Greek words *ithy*, meaning "straight," and *phallo*, meaning "penis"

ITHYPHALLOPHOBIA is the fear of seeing or having an erect penis. While an erection is a normal and natural occurrence for most men, there are both women and men who are petrified of an engorged member. The phobia is not necessarily limited to fear of an exposed erect penis, but may include fear at seeing one through clothing. This phobia originates from a strict or religious upbringing in which it was taught that sex is dirty or wrong. A woman may feel threatened by a man with an erection, while a man may feel like a sinner for having one. Sufferers may also have been the victim of sexual abuse. In its broader sense, ithyphallophobia is a fear of masculinity, suffered by women who fear male aggression. Men who suffer from the phobia avoid wearing sweatpants and other light fabrics, especially in public, and feel embarrassed and vulnerable at the thought of inadvertently displaying their clothed man-bulge. Sufferers of both genders avoid social settings where an erect penis could be encountered (the Playboy Mansion, for instance), and places where men are likely to wear revealing clothing, like the gym or beach. Sexual liaisons may be avoided by both genders. Therapeutic assistance is the most common form of treatment for this condition. Medication treats both the symptoms of anxiety and sometimes has the added side effect of lowering libido in men. Just be sure you don't accidentally take one of those little blue pills.

THINGS TO AVOID: Viagra; thinking about anything relating to sex; men.

|||| Phobia Trivia ||||

Ithyphallophobia is also known as medorthophobia (from the Greek word *ortho*, meaning "erect") and phallophobia (from the Greek word *phallo*, meaning "penis"). Yinjingphobia is the fear of the word "penis."

|||| Statistics ||||

The American actor and TV host Jonah Falcon is said to have the world's largest penis, measuring 13.5 inches long when erect. He has never been invited to a gathering of ithyphallophobes.

Is for Judeophobia

Judeophobia

MEANING: fear of Jews

ORIGIN: the Latin word *judaeus*, meaning "Jewish"

JUDEOPHOBIA is the fear of Jewish people, and might include extreme hostility to and prejudice against Jews. Sometimes referred to as anti-Semitism, the persecution of Jews extends back to Hellenistic Egypt, when a Jewish temple was destroyed in Elephantine in 410 BC. From there it spread to Palestine and then the Roman Empire. There are a number of stereotypes about Jews that contribute to the condition, including religious notions about the killing of Christ, the economic association of Jews with money and banking, and other racist ideas perpetuated about Jews to stoke racial and cultural resentment. Judeophobia manifests in many ways, including both discrimination against individuals and attacks on entire communities. Many judeophobes, however, simply avoid Jewish people.

THINGS TO AVOID: Israel; synagogues.

|||| Phobia Trivia ||||

The word "judeophobia" first appeared in the German pamphlet *Auto-Emancipation* in 1882. Anti-Semitism is considered a form of racism; instances of persecution throughout history include the Rhineland massacres before the First Crusade in 1096, the Edict of Expulsion from England in 1290, the 1391 massacre of Spanish Jews, the Spanish Inquisition, the expulsion from Spain in 1492, the Cossack massacres in Ukraine from 1648 to 1657, the anti-Jewish initiatives in the Russian Empire between 1821 and 1906, the Dreyfus Affair in France, and, most notoriously, the Holocaust in German-occupied Europe by Nazis between 1941 and 1945.

Statistics

Around 6 million Jews (two-thirds of the Jewish population of Europe) were murdered during the Holocaust, making it statistically the worst genocide in history.

Is for
Kinemortophobia

Kakologophobia

MEANING: fear of swear words

ORIGIN: the Greek words *kakos*, meaning "bad," and *logos*, meaning "word"

KAKOLOGOPHOBIA is the extreme fear of swear words, both using them and hearing them. The condition is incited by trauma, like getting yelled at for swearing or accidentally using lewd language in front of a grandmother, resulting in extreme embarrassment. Being the target of a barrage of particularly aggressive invective can also result in kakologophobia. Sufferers do whatever they can to avoid foul language, staying out of bars and away from habitual swearers. Exposure to profanity can cause profuse sweating, shaking, and vomiting; sufferers may flee the scene or cover their ears in defense. Those with a severe case of the phobia go so far as to avoid cursing that they end up reclusive. Alone, the kakologophobe can live in relative safety from any offensive language—as long as they don't accidentally stub a toe.

THINGS TO AVOID: sailors, so the saying goes; comedy clubs; a lot of films; some rap songs; television after 9 p.m.

||||| Phobia Trivia |||||

Kakologophobia is sometimes known as deprecophobia, and is a branch of logophobia, which is the fear of any word. There are a number of more specific swearing-related fears: mugouphobia (the fear of the word "bitch"), katourophobia (the fear of the word "piss"), skataphobia (the fear of the word "shit"), and zomaiphobia (the fear of the word "fuck").

There are around 150 swear words in the English language. A 2009 analysis of recorded conversations published in *Perspectives on Psychological Science* found that an average of 80 to 90 words that a person speaks each day are swear words.

Kathisophobia

MEANING: fear of sitting down

ORIGIN: the Greek word *kathiso*, meaning "to sit" or "sitting"

Known also as thaasophobia or cathisophobia, KATHISO-PHOBIA is the extreme fear of sitting down. It often arises when the act of sitting is painful or uncomfortable. Some elderly people sit for long periods because they are immobile, causing pain and distress that can lead to kathisophobia. Children forced to sit obediently in class can experience feelings of being trapped or unduly controlled, which can trigger the condition. A traumatic experience, like being made to sit on the floor of a bank for a long period during a hostage situation, can also instill this fear (among others). With symptoms like nausea, inability to speak, detachment from reality, and panic attacks, kathisophobes will do whatever they can to avoid sitting. Given that sitting is a key part of everyday life—playing a role in education, most jobs, many social interactions, travel, and the vast majority of pastimes—it goes without saying that life for the kathisophobe can be rather difficult. Counseling can sometimes help.

THINGS TO AVOID: nearly all forms of travel except for hang gliding and hot air balloons (unless you're a globophobe); horseback riding; educational facilities; coffeehouses; office jobs; living rooms; tables.

|||| **Phobia Trivia** ||||

Stasiphobia is the fear of standing. Presumably, someone who suffers from both stasiphobia and kathisophobia has no option but to lay in bed all day while the rest of us work.

|||| **Statistics** ||||

On average, Americans sit for around nine hours per day.

Katsaridaphobia

MEANING: fear of cockroaches

ORIGIN: the Greek word *katsarida*, meaning "cockroach"

KATSARIDAPHOBIA is the morbid and irrational fear of cockroaches. While most people find the animal somewhat disgusting, katsaridaphobes take it to the extreme. The primary cause of this phobia is the association of cockroaches with disease. Of the 4,600 species of cockroach, about 30 share human habitats, feeding on scraps of food and carrying pathogenic microbes that can lead to allergic reactions, illness, and disease. People with a horrifying cockroach-related experience are more likely to develop katsaridaphobia. For others, the unpleasant creatures evoking feelings of disgust and repulsion can result in the condition. Katsaridaphobia can lead to obsessive-compulsive disorder, characterized by constantly cleaning the house and spraying insecticides to deter the creatures. Panic attacks are also common in some sufferers. Cockroaches can live for up to a month without food and can withstand many times the radiation levels that humans can. So, in the event that you find yourself the only survivor in a postapocalyptic world, you'd better hope you're not a katsaridaphobe, as you won't be totally alone. And, as most people know, just because they aren't visible, doesn't mean they're not there.

THINGS TO AVOID: nearly all houses late at night; the traditional Spanish folk song "La Cucaracha"; postapocalyptic worlds; the humid South, where it is common for cockroaches to fly.

||||| Phobia Trivia |||||

While considered disgusting in Western culture (and it's probably best not to read this if you are a katsaridaphobe), cockroaches are eaten in Mexico, Thailand, Taiwan, and China. In fact, in China, they are fried in hot oil, making them crispy on the outside and soft in the middle. Scarlett Johansson is katsaridaphobic. Katsaridaphobes do have something in common with cockroaches: Most cockroaches have anthropophobia (the fear of humans), hiding away to clean themselves if we touch them.

||||| Statistics |||||

A cockroach can hold its breath for 40 minutes, survive being submerged in water for 30 minutes, and live for seven days without its head. The world's largest cockroach, from South America, is 6 inches long and has a 1-foot wingspan.

Kinemortophobia

MEANING: fear of zombies

ORIGIN: the Greek word *kine*, meaning "to move," and the Latin word *mort*, meaning "dead"

KINEMORTOPHOBIA, literally a phobia of the "walking dead," is the fear of zombies or being turned into a zombie. Strange as it may sound, it is not only a very real phobia, but also a fairly common one; hundreds of thousands of people of all ages are thought to be affected. The fear often results in nightmares or an inability to sleep, which can lead to stress, depression, and withdrawal from society. Just someone doing an impression of a zombie (arms out in front, stiff walk, incoherent mumbling and groaning) can cause kinemortophobes to experience a panic attack. Fear of zombies may come from our evolutionary fear of cannibalism, or be traced back to childhood trauma: getting scared by zombie movies or a Halloween costume. The phobia is exacerbated by the ubiquity of zombie imagery in popular culture. As with any phobia of a mythical creature, kinemortophobia can be difficult to admit to, especially for an educated adult, but sufferers are encouraged to talk about their problem with a mental health professional (and just hope like hell they're not a zombie in disguise).

THINGS TO AVOID: *The Walking Dead* (obviously); playing video games like *Resident Evil* and *Plants vs. Zombies*; *Night of the Living Dead*; Halloween; The Cranberries song "Zombie."

Phobia Trivia

The modern image of the zombie originated in West African voodoo lore. American actress and singer Emma Roberts has been a kinemortophobe since watching the Brad Pitt zombie film *World War Z* in 2013. It was Victor Halperin's 1932 film *White Zombie* that started things on the big screen, often cited as the first zombie film. The bad news for kinemortophobes is that 280 such movies have been made since the turn of the century. But not all hope is lost. On their website, the Centers for Disease Control and Prevention has published helpful directions on how to proceed in the event of a zombie apocalypse.

|||| Statistics ||||

In a 2015 poll of 1,000 adults by YouGov, 2 percent of Americans said that if an apocalypse was going to happen, it would be at the hands of zombies. 28 percent thought it would be nuclear war.

Koinoniphobia

MEANING: fear of rooms

ORIGIN: the Greek word *koini*, meaning "frequent" or "shared"

KOINONIPHOBIA is the intense fear of rooms and is closely related to claustrophobia (the fear of enclosed spaces). This bizarre condition is often triggered by an obsessive desire to have a perfect room; anything falling short becomes a source of fear. Cracking paint or squeaky floors in a room are indicative of imperfection and can lead to extreme anxiety for the koinoniphobe. Concerns about paranormal activity or what may be happening on the other side of the wall can also incite the phobia. The more rooms a house has, the scarier for the koin-oniphobe, who often prefers to live in a single-roomed house, or may even choose homelessness to avoid rooms altogether. Sufferers avoid entering buildings and other people's houses; entering a room can cause shaking, parched mouth, sweating, and an inability to communicate. These symptoms can be detrimental to the professional lives of koinoniphobes—rare is the occupation that doesn't require at least the occasional entry into a room. Personal relationships also usually suffer from the reluctance to meet anyone in a room. Thus, forming any kind of meaningful sexual relationship is also very difficult for koinoniphobes.

THINGS TO AVOID: houses, buildings, and workplaces; the film *Panic Room*; the Winchester Mystery House; television shows and films that take place indoors.

|||| Phobia Trivia ||||

Koinoniphobia is also closely related to oikophobia (the fear of being in a house) and cleithrophobia (the fear of being trapped).

|||| Statistics ||||

According to *Guinness World Records*, the largest palace in the world is the Forbidden City in Beijing, which has 8,886 rooms. The White House has 132 rooms.

Koumpounophobia

MEANING: fear of buttons

ORIGIN: the modern Greek word *koumpouno*, meaning "to button," from the ancient Greek word *kuamos*, meaning "bean"

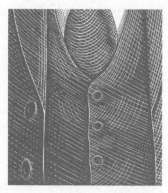

KOUMPOUNOPHOBIA is the fear of buttons, both standalone buttons and those affixed to apparel. While the thought or sight of buttons can trigger extreme anxiety in sufferers, the fear can vary depending on the type and style of button encountered. Some koumpounophobes are afraid of all types of buttons, while for others, fear might depend on the texture of the button. Metal buttons, like those that appear on jeans, are not as commonly feared as plastic ones. Some people believe buttons are dirty and are more afraid of old buttons, while others worry about the chance that they may accidentally swallow or inhale a small button. The fear of buttons is usually related to a trauma like choking on a button or being mistreated by someone who wore clothes with prominent or distinctive buttons. Koumpounophobia can affect the sufferer's ability to attend formal gatherings, weddings, funerals, and christenings, and can even limit a person's ability to work. The sufferer can't get dressed up and, while antidepressants have been known to help, many koumpounophobes are too embarrassed to discuss their condition and consequently lose contact with family and friends.

THINGS TO AVOID: formal gatherings; elevators; accidentally spilling Grandma's dish of filthy old buttons all over yourself; The Pussycat Dolls 2006 song "Buttons."

||||| Phobia Trivia |||||

Neil Gaiman's 2002 horror novel *Coraline* (which was adapted into a film) deals with this concept. The lead character, after discovering a parallel world with sinister people who resemble her parents but have buttons for eyes, develops an acute case of koumpounophobia. But while the condition is not widely known (or at least not widely discussed), its existence has, in fact, changed the world as we know it. Apple cofounder Steve Jobs suffered from button phobia, which inspired his creation of the iPhone's buttonless touchscreen, which has revolutionized the lives of many people, especially those with big fingers. A fear of buttons was also the reason for Steve's preference for turtlenecks.

||||| Statistics |||||

Koumpounophobia is a rare phobia that affects around 1 in 75,000 people.

Kynophobia

MEANING: fear of rabies

ORIGIN: the Greek word *kyno*, meaning "dog"

KYNOPHOBIA is the fear of rabies or of becoming mad from its contraction. More prevalent in women than in men, this rare phobia usually arises from a frightening childhood encounter with a dog or having to get a rabies injection because of a dog bite. Stories or films about vicious dogs can also lead to kyno-phobia, as can the knowledge of what rabies does to a person. With symptoms that include violent movements, dizziness, nausea, fear of water, confusion, loss of consciousness, and, in all but 14 cases, death, there is good reason to be fearful of this viral disease. Kynophobes often express visible fear in the presence of any animal they suspect to be rabid, avoiding wooded areas and zoos. Counseling and cognitive behavioral therapy are the most common methods for overcoming the condition. In a twist of irony, kynophobia, without treatment, can lead to a number of the same symptoms as rabies.

THINGS TO AVOID: most of Mexico, Central America, South America, Asia, and Africa; *Cujo* (book and film).

|||| Phobia Trivia ||||

Kynophobia is also called cynophobia and is related to hydro-phobia (the fear of water or rabies), hydrophobophobia (the fear of rabies), and lyssophobia (the fear of going insane or getting rabies).

|||| Statistics ||||

Rabies causes more than 55,000 deaths worldwide each year.

Kyphophobia

MEANING: fear of stooping

ORIGIN: the Greek word *kypho*, meaning "bent" or "humped"

KYPHOPHOBIA is the fear of stooping. Stooping or bending is a daily occurrence for most people, making life incredibly difficult for the kyphophobe. The condition usually stems from a traumatic event, like severe back pain, paralysis, or having been trampled by an unruly mob while in a stooped position. Difficulties with balance can also lead to a fear of stooping. Another cause is the belief that too much stooping can result in an inability to stand up straight again. Kyphophobes experience extreme anxiety in any stooping-related situation and avoid bending down to pick things up, tie a shoelace, or look for a lost item under furniture. The thought of stooping or seeing someone else stoop causes tremors, nausea, and weeping. Learning that stooping in moderation is typically not harmful is the most effective technique to deal with this condition. Otherwise life for the sufferer can be both difficult and messy, with dropped objects strewn all over the house. Untreated, the condition can lead to unduly long showers should the sufferer happen to drop the soap—perhaps it was a kyphophobe who invented the nifty soap on a rope.

THINGS TO AVOID: *The Hunchback of Notre Dame* (book and film); dropping anything; picking anything up; medieval castles; shoelaces.

||||| Phobia Trivia |||||

The expression "have a hunch" takes its origins from gambling in early 20th-century America and the most famous stoopers of them all, hunchbacks. There is a centuries-old superstition that hunchbacks are possessed by the devil, who gave them the power to foretell the future. Gamblers, notoriously superstitious, believed that rubbing the hump of a hunchback before placing a bet would bring them good fortune.

The 1996 film *The Hunchback of Notre Dame* grossed $325 million worldwide, making it the fifth highest-grossing film for that year.

L

Is for Linonophobia

Laliophobia

MEANING: fear of speaking

ORIGIN: the Greek word *lal*, meaning "speech"

LALIOPHOBIA is the fear of speaking. While many people are afraid of talking in front of a crowd, sufferers of this social phobia are afraid of speaking to people in any situation. Laliophobes are terrified that they may stutter, babble, or fumble over or forget their words. This fear can arise from an embarrassing mispronunciation or humiliating verbal gaff that resulted in ridicule. The idea of speaking to people can trigger dry mouth, loss of voice, a lump in the throat, and other symptoms that make it even more difficult to speak. Nausea and a feeling of complete panic can also result, neither conducive to eloquence. Laliophobes avoid speaking to other people, often becoming withdrawn and unwilling to attend social gatherings. Speech therapy is a common treatment; behavioral therapy is also used. As speaking is a major part of everyday existence, life can be tough for the laliophobe. If therapy doesn't work, there's always the option of becoming a monk and taking a vow of silence.

THINGS TO AVOID: interacting in virtually any social setting; discussion groups; speeches; meeting people in the street; buying things in shops; ordering things in bars or restaurants; most workplaces.

||||| Phobia Trivia |||||

Laliophobia is also known as lalophobia and is closely related to glossophobia, which is the fear of public speaking, a common affliction. So common is it, in fact, that some surveys have shown that most people are more afraid of speaking in public than they are of death, which means that, at a funeral, they'd rather be in the coffin than giving the eulogy.

|||| Statistics ||||

It is estimated that 75 percent of Americans are afraid of public speaking.

Lepidopterophobia

MEANING: fear of butterflies

ORIGIN: the Greek word *lepidoptera*, which is the group or class of insects that includes butterflies, moths, skippers, and other winged insects

LEPIDOPTEROPHOBIA is the fear of butterflies. While many people marvel at the beauty of these harmless insects, sufferers of this condition are afraid of the rapid movement, flashing colors, and creepy-crawliness of butterflies. Many lepidopterophobes are also scared of other winged insects, as well as birds. The fact that butterflies sometimes travel in swarms adds to the fear, the large quantity of animals increasing the perceived danger. In addition to feelings of intense disgust at the sight of a butterfly, sufferers also experience nausea, shaking, and desperation to flee. More extreme lepidopterophobes imagine being attacked by the dainty insects, plagued by the thought like a horror scene on loop. And while there are no recorded cases of butterflies causing harm to humans, that doesn't mean it hasn't happened or isn't possible. Aside from exposure therapy, the best form of treatment is talking through your fear with friends and loved ones, if, that is, you're willing to admit to it.

THINGS TO AVOID: gardens; parks; zoos; flower shops; the outdoors.

Phobia Trivia

Lepidopterophobia is closely linked with entomophobia, which is the fear of insects, and mottephobia, the fear of moths. Australian actress Nicole Kidman suffers from lepidopterophobia.

Statistics

There are around 18,500 known species of butterflies across the world.

Leukophobia

MEANING: fear of the color white

ORIGIN: the Greek word *leuko*, meaning "white"

LEUKOPHOBIA is the morbid fear of the color white. While for many people white represents peace, purity, and cleanliness, for leukophobes it is a source of terror. Snow is often at the source of this fear: Sufferers may have had a bad experience with snow, like a skiing accident or getting stuck in a snow drift. The association of trauma with the color white leads to the phobia. A fear of marriage can also lead to an onset of leukophobia because of the traditional white dress. Others fear the color for no apparent reason at all. With white things all around us, including clouds, snow, clothing, and paper, life for the leukophobe can be challenging. The sufferer wears colorful clothes, lives in a dark or colorful house, avoids white buildings, refuses to take white pills, and won't drink milk, unless it's chocolate milk (that last part isn't so bad). Just the mention of the word "white" causes tremors, restlessness, and a feeling of being enclosed or trapped. Leukophobia may lead to a fixation on pale skin and an association of whiteness with ghosts. This can be of particular concern for leukophobes who also suffer from phasmophobia (the fear of ghosts). Treatment includes behavioral therapy to address the root cause of the problem, and teaching the patient that the color white is nowhere near as scary as its opposite.

THINGS TO AVOID: weddings; most clouds; most stereotypical ghosts; Billy Idol's song "White Wedding"; Cat Stevens' song "Into White"; Procol Harum's song "A Whiter Shade of Pale"; snow; paper; bed linens, towels, and clothing; vanilla ice cream; a lot of people named "White"; *Snow White and the Seven Dwarfs* (books and films).

|||| Phobia Trivia ||||

Leukophobia is a subclass of chromophobia, which is the fear of colors. The fear of the color black is known as melanophobia.

|||| Statistics ||||

The Salar de Uyuni in Bolivia is the world's largest salt flat, a 4,086 square-mile stretch of flat, salt-covered land that is nearly pure white as far as the eye can see.

Ligyrophobia

MEANING: fear of loud noises

ORIGIN: the Greek word *ligyro*, meaning "sharp"

LIGYROPHOBIA is the fear of or aversion to loud noises, and is closely related to (although not to be confused with) acousticophobia (the fear of noise in general) and phonophobia (the fear of voices or one's own voice). The phobia is commonly triggered by a sudden loud sound—an alarm, fireworks, or balloon popping—and is a fairly common phobia that affects people of all ages. While most people are startled by a loud, blaring noise, the reaction only lasts a few seconds, whereas ligyrophobes are rendered helpless. They fear devices that emit loud noises, including televisions and stereo speakers, and that exposure to loud noise will damage their eardrums or cause other injury. Conditions like autism and adrenal insufficiency can contribute to the phobia, as can a traumatic experience involving loud noise. To some extent, however, fear of loud noises is innate in humans: Sharp and alarming noises caused our early ancestors to take cover for safety. Nausea, fainting, and sweating are common side effects, as is the tendency to avoid all loud environments. Exposure therapy is the principal method of treatment, offering small doses of noise before eventually subjecting the patient to what would have been crippling levels of sound. This technique has had varied success.

THINGS TO AVOID: parades; carnivals; rock concerts; sports stadiums; fireworks spectacles; Fourth of July festivities; balloons; firearms; cities; restaurants; bars; cars; planes; trains;

pretty much any fun activity that occurs outside the house where other people will be present.

The ligyrophobe's aversion to loud environments often leads to the development of enochlophobia, the fear of large crowds or gatherings, as these situations are usually accompanied by lots of noise. Ligyrophobia is also known as sonophobia.

Scientists believe that the 1883 Krakatoa volcanic eruption in Indonesia is the loudest sound ever heard. It ruptured the eardrums of people 40 miles away, traveled around the world almost four times, and was clearly heard 3,000 miles away, including in the middle of Australia.

Linonophobia

MEANING: fear of string

ORIGIN: the Greek word *lino*, meaning "string"

LINONOPHOBIA is the abnormal fear of string, rope, yarn, twine, or thread. Many people with this phobia associate string with being tied up or restrained, and may have been tied up as punishment as a child. The fear might also be developed from watching a film or television show in which someone was kidnapped and tied up. Seeing or even thinking about string causes heart palpitations, nausea, fainting, and an uncontrollable urge to flee. The typical linonophobe has a hard time dealing with clothes, carpets, blankets, textiles, and a multitude of other everyday objects made from stringy fibers. Tooth-flossing is totally out of the question for genuine linonophobes. Therapy has been shown to reduce the anxiety caused by this phobia—just make sure the therapist is wearing slip-on shoes.

THINGS TO AVOID: kites; yo-yos; macramé; the cat's-cradle game; string theory; cute cats playing with balls of yarn; getting strung along or doing the stringing; guitars (and the rest of the string section); tennis, squash, badminton and other racquet sports; shoelaces.

|||| Phobia Trivia ||||

Linonophobes tend not to discriminate and usually fear string of all colors.

|||| Statistics ||||

The largest ball of string was made in Texas between 1989 and 1992. It had a diameter of 13 feet 2.5 inches, and a circumference of 41 feet 6 inches.

Liticaphobia

MEANING: fear of lawsuits

ORIGIN: the Greek word *litigo*, meaning "litigate"

Also known as litigophobia, LITICAPHOBIA is the persistent and irrational fear of lawsuits or being sued. While most people are apprehensive at the realistic prospect of being sued, liticaphobes live in fear of litigation at all times. The phobia can be caused by a past lawsuit or being close to someone who was sued. Liticaphobia is more prevalent in countries where litigation is common, and where movies and television shows depicting courtroom dramas are popular. The condition is also related to a lack of understanding of the law and the rules of court. For other sufferers, fear of the consequences of being sued—including financial loss, jail time, or execution—is the source of the fear. Liticaphobes are generally law-abiding citizens, worried about avoiding a lawsuit, and exhibit anxiety, tremors, and an incredible urge to flee if faced with a lawyer or courtroom. In addition to psychotherapy, treatment includes educating the patient about the realities of the legal system: Television shows and films are exaggerated for entertainment purposes, not everyone who gets sued loses, and lawsuits don't typically result in the defendant's execution. Advising the liticaphobe not to flee if they are summoned to court also helps the sufferer to avoid the very consequences they fear, namely, losing the case and having to pay money or suffer imprisonment or execution.

THINGS TO AVOID: *Law & Order*, *Suits*, *Goliath*, and other TV procedural dramas; litigious people; John Grisham novels; Jonathan Lee Riches (see Phobia Trivia below); Donald Trump (see Statistics on next page).

|||| Phobia Trivia ||||

Thought to be the most litigious man in the world, since 2006 Jonathan Lee Riches has filed more than 2,600 lawsuits against famous defendants including George W. Bush, Steve Jobs, Britney Spears, and Martha Stewart, as well as Plato, Nostradamus, Che Guevara, the Lincoln Memorial, and the Eiffel Tower. Upon hearing that *Guinness World Records* planned to name him as "The Most Litigious Man," he did what he does best—sued them.

As of 2016, Donald Trump and his businesses had been involved in over 3,500 legal actions in federal and state courts—let's hope he's not a liticaphobe.

Logizomechanophobia

MEANING: fear of computers

ORIGIN: the Greek words *log*, meaning "talk" or "word," and *machano*, meaning "machine"

Also known as cyberphobia, LOGIZOMECHANOPHOBIA is the fear of computers. Difficulty learning to use a computer and the confusing concepts and terminology associated with computers can cause this modern-day phobia. Losing a job to automation or having to change the way you work because of technological advances can also lead to logizomechanophobia, as can having your computer hacked. Symptoms include shortness of breath, tremors, and a feeling of extreme isolation. The mere sight or thought of the mechanical objects instills terror, and logizomechanophobes do whatever than can to avoid computers. Should the phobia strike suddenly while working on a computer, the sufferer is unlikely to back up their files before fleeing the scene. Given the rise of technology in the modern workplace, life for logizomechanophobes can be incredibly taxing. Treatment involves teaching the sufferer that today's computers are much easier to use than their 1970s predecessors and can make life a lot easier when used correctly.

THINGS TO AVOID: desktop computers; laptop computers; tablet computers; computer keyboards; computer mice; Silicon Valley; the film *Electric Dreams*.

Logizomechanophobia is sometimes considered a branch of mediaphobia (the fear of the media), and a branch of technophobia (the fear of technology). There are also a number of more specific computer-related fears: zhuojphobia (the fear of desktop computers), bijixphobia (the fear of laptop computers), pingbophobia (the fear of tablet computers), ordclaviphobia (the fear of computer keyboards), and osouriphobia (the fear of computer mice, not to be confused with musophobia [the fear of actual mice]).

Work on the first substantial computer, known as ENIAC, began in 1943 and took three years to finish. The computer occupied about 1,800 square feet, used about 18,000 vacuum tubes, and weighed almost 50 tons.

Lutraphobia

MEANING: fear of otters

ORIGIN: the Greek word *lutra*, meaning "otter"

LUTRAPHOBIA is the irrational and persistent fear of otters. While many find otters cute and playful, for lutraphobes they are a source of terror; sufferers of this condition avoid swimming in or going near bodies of water where otters may lurk. Fear of otters is not without reason: When startled or provoked, otters can become aggressive and even attack with their sharp teeth and claws, powerful bite, and a thick and luxurious coat that, though it feels nice, only aids in their protection. Powerful swimmers, they can hold their breath for up to eight minutes, making them a formidable adversary under water. In addition, otters actually use tools, employing a rock as a hammer to break open shells; who's to say they wouldn't use it as a weapon as well? Staying away from oceans and rivers to avoid otters altogether is the best treatment. Unfortunately, if you do come face to face with an aggressive otter, the news is not good: U.S. and international law protects otters, the largest member of the weasel family, so fighting the carnivorous mammals is out of the question.

THINGS TO AVOID: Alaska, home to approximately 90 percent of the world's sea otters; zoos; Hermione Granger's patronus; rivers; oceans.

|||| Phobia Trivia ||||

A group of swimming otters is called a romp, bevy, or lodge, while a group of resting otters is called a raft because of their tendency to cling to seaweed and float along together.

|||| Statistics ||||

River otters are much smaller (averaging 10 to 30 pounds) than their seafaring cousins, who can weigh up to 90 pounds. That said, giant 6-foot otters exist in some remote river systems of South America, hunting in packs and even taking on crocodiles.

Is for Melophobia

Macrophobia

MEANING: fear of long waits

ORIGIN: the Greek word *macro*, meaning "long"

MACROPHOBIA is the unnatural fear of long waits. While many people hate waiting, macrophobes actually fear it. Sufferers may have had impatience that led to panic and the onset of macrophobia. Missing a flight due to a long wait at airport security, for example, can cause this phobia. Waiting can also give rise to feelings of frustration and a lack of control, resulting in an urge to flee, fainting, and the sensation that the walls are closing in. Everyday activities like going to the doctor, going to the bank, and shopping become untenable. To avoid these unendurable waits, macrophobes refuse to leave the house and instead buy everything online. If this is your reality, be sure that your internet signal is strong—waiting for a website to load is the most unbearable wait of them all.

THINGS TO AVOID: government agencies; call centers; Disney World; the *Seinfeld* episode "The Chinese Restaurant" where the characters experience a very long wait; traffic jams; restaurants that don't take reservations.

Phobia Trivia

According to a 2014 study by the Texas A&M Transportation Institute and data company INRIX, Americans spend 6.9 billion hours a year waiting in traffic, which equates to 42 hours a year for every commuter. That's a lot of time idling, in addition to the $1,400 for gas.

When Sony released the PlayStation 3 in 2006, gamers across America waited in lines for up to three days to purchase it.

Mageirocophobia

MEANING: fear of cooking

ORIGIN: the Greek word *mageiros*, meaning "chef" or "butcher"

MAGEIROCOPHOBIA is the intense fear of cooking. While cooking shows and celebrity chefs are becoming more popular, they are a source of terror for the mageirocophobe, who can neither stand the heat nor to be in the kitchen at all. Predominantly found in adults, this phobia is commonly based in the fear that undercooked or improperly pre-pared food can cause illness or disease. Performance anxiety about making bad food is another common cause, as is fear of kitchen accidents, complex recipes, unhealthy ingredients, and overeating. A culinary mishap, like inadvertently poison-ing a dinner guest, might incite the phobia. Mageirocophobes are also fearful of other people's cooking. Constant culinary dread means that sufferers eat very little or not at all, or stick to packaged foods and snacks. The resultant unhealthy diet can lead to hypertension, diabetes, and obesity. Treatment involves counseling and educating the patient on basic cooking techniques, ingredients, and knife skills.

THINGS TO AVOID: Nigella Lawson; Gordon Ramsay; Jamie Oliver; Food Network; kitchens in homes, restaurants, cafés, and fast-food establishments; the cookbook section of the bookstore.

|||| Phobia Trivia ||||

According to a 2011 Oxfam study in which 16,000 people from 17 countries were surveyed, the world's top three foods to cook were pasta, meat, and rice. In the United States, the top three were pizza, steak, and chicken.

|||| Statistics ||||

English chef Jamie Oliver is the world's richest celebrity chef, worth an estimated $372 million. Nobu Matsuhisa is second, with a fortune estimated at $200 million, and Gordon Ramsay is third, at $190 million.

Medomalacuphobia

MEANING: fear of losing an erection

ORIGIN: the Greek word *malaco*, meaning "softness"

MEDOMALACUPHOBIA is the debilitating fear of losing an erection. Erectile dysfunction is a common issue for men, and can cause embarrassment and feelings of inadequacy. But medomalacuphobia is more than common performance anxiety—it's a major fear. This phobia is linked to fear of ridicule, especially in men who have been mocked for their vulnerability and inadequacy in the past. The fear itself can lead to erectile dysfunction, leaving the sufferer feeling worthless, defective, and unworthy of love and sex. When a downturn (so to speak) occurs, sufferers tremble, sweat excessively, panic, or flee, resigning themselves to a life of frustrated isolation. Coming to terms with erectile dysfunction can be extremely difficult for the medomalacuphobe, who may live in fear rather than speak openly about it. Sufferers may resort to medications like Viagra. Unlike men, women are not susceptible to this phobia. While performance problems may be a source of disappointment and frustration for a female partner, the condition is specific to men who fear losing an erection.

THINGS TO AVOID: situations where erections are expected to be maintained, principally in bed with a sexual partner.

Phobia Trivia

The well-known erectile dysfunction drug Viagra, manufactured by the pharmaceutical company Pfizer, was initially developed to treat heart conditions; the effects it had on other parts of the body arose during testing. Medomalacuphobia is related to ithyphallophobia (the fear of seeing, thinking about, or having an erect penis), medorthophobia (the fear of an erect penis), and phallophobia (general fear of the penis).

Statistics

It is estimated that 5 percent of men over 40 have complete erectile dysfunction, as do 15 percent of men over 70.

Melophobia

MEANING: fear of music

ORIGIN: the Greek word *melodia*, meaning "music"

MELOPHOBIA is the fear of music. Calming and uplifting for many people, music is a source of fear and anxiety for others. Just as music can evoke a pleasant memory from the time we first heard it, it can also awaken memories of dread and torment, causing a person to avoid a specific song or genre of music, or music altogether. These melophobic people listen to very little or no music, which can make their lives very difficult. Just going to a grocery store or restaurant can lead to breathlessness, tremors, panic attacks, and an uncontrollable desire to flee. Workplaces that play music become impossible, as does attending social functions and events where the joyous sounds of music fill the air. Therapy is the main method for treating this phobia, with the goal of teaching the melophobe that music can be enjoyable and is not inherently evil and there is nothing to fear. (Excluding Slayer and other thrash metal bands. They actually are pretty damn scary.)

THINGS TO AVOID: cafés; bookstores; television; stereos; portable music players; radio; the album *Melophobia* by American rock band Cage the Elephant; bars and clubs; concerts; lots of famous people; Christmastime; birthday parties.

|||| Phobia Trivia ||||

Melophobia is also known as the unimaginatively named musicophobia.

By album sales, the top five selling music artists of all time are The Beatles, Elvis Presley, Michael Jackson, Madonna, and Elton John.

Metathesiophobia

MEANING: fear of change

ORIGIN: the Greek word *meta*, meaning "change"

METATHESIOPHOBIA is the fear of change. Some experts believe this fear to be inherent: an internal predisposition to resisting change and feeling in control. While it is normal to dislike change, the metathesiophobe has a persistent and intense fear of it, sometimes brought on by moving many times as a child, the loss of a parent, or other unwanted lifestyle changes. The phobia is also thought to be related to obsessive-compulsive disorder. Metathesiophobes feel the need to have complete control over their lives, and thus refuse to introduce new things or disrupt their routine. Sometimes it's the fear of failure that keeps sufferers from doing anything differently; they go to great lengths to avoid change, including lying, making excuses, and ostracizing friends. This behavior can lead to a disastrous personal and professional life, as well as suicidal thoughts. The deeply embedded aversion to change makes seeking help extremely difficult. Most medical professionals agree that overcoming a fear of change with therapy is essential to leading a happy and healthy life. In some cases, however, the condition is thought to be a symptom of a more serious mental disorder and requires medication.

THINGS TO AVOID: certain Bob Dylan and David Bowie songs; deciduous trees; annual flowers; the seasons; the moon and its phases; caterpillars and butterflies; most other things in life.

Benjamin Franklin, who once said, "When you're finished changing, you're finished," was not a sufferer of metathesiophobia. Metathesiophobia is often linked with tropophobia, which is the fear of moving. It can also be known as neophobia, kainolophobia, or kainophobia (the fear of anything new), cainophobia or cainotophobia (the fear of newness or novelty), and prosophobia (the fear of progress). Plenty of options for those who like to change things up.

|||| Statistics ||||

Many countries have changed names throughout history. Belgium has had six names. Let's hope there aren't many Belgian metathesiophobes.

Methyphobia

MEANING: fear of alcohol

ORIGIN: the Greek word *methy*, meaning "alcohol"

METHYPHOBIA is the fear of alcohol, including beer, wine, and spirits. Alcohol's effects on the brain can lead to a loss of inhibition, resulting in bad judgments that can be life changing.

Methyphobia is often caused by the fear of losing control after drinking, or a fear of being in the presence of someone else who does. Past alcohol-related violence or abuse, or the negative impacts of a drunk-driving accident, are common causes of this condition. Religious beliefs and genetics can also play a role in triggering methyphobia. Sufferers avoid drinking alcohol, as well as anyone who drinks it, and often actively avoid any situation where they might be exposed to alcohol, like parties, family gatherings, and weddings. Going to bars and restaurants is out of the question; even the smell of alcohol causes perspiration, shaking, and nausea. Most cases of methyphobia are self-diagnosed. Treatment ranges from hypnotherapy and meditation to support groups with like-minded people. Exposure therapy is also commonly used to treat the condition. This involves exposing the methyphobe to images before introducing them to situations where others are drinking. The technique rarely involves forcing anyone to drink copious quantities of alcohol, which would do little more than make the sufferer temporarily forget about their phobia.

THINGS TO AVOID: bars; restaurants; cafés; grocery stores; social events; Eastern Europe; college fraternities and sororities.

||||| Phobia Trivia |||||

Methyphobia is also known as potophobia (from the Latin word *poto*, meaning "drink"), and is closely related to dipsophobia (the fear of drinking).

||||| Statistics |||||

Here are the top 10 biggest drinking nations in the world, with the average number of liters of pure alcohol consumed per person each year: Belarus (17.5), Moldova (16.8), Lithuania

(15.4), Russia (15.1), Romania (14.4), Ukraine (13.9), Andorra (13.8), Hungary (13.3), Czech Republic (13), and Slovakia (13). It seems there aren't a lot of methyphobes in Eastern Europe.

Metrophobia

MEANING: fear of poetry

ORIGIN: the Greek word *metron*, meaning "measure"

METROPHOBIA is the overwhelming fear of poetry. Poetry has been recited since the ancient Greeks and is considered one of the most beautiful and rewarding written forms. Metrophobes, however, fear and loathe poetry and avoid writing, reading, or listening to poems. The phobia frequently develops in school-children who are forced by overzealous teachers to study poetry in search of obscure and often nonexistent meaning. The fear is also brought on by the content of poetry. Student sufferers may refuse to participate in English classes, or begin skipping school altogether. The anxiety over poetry can become so strong that it leads to didaskaleinophobia (the fear of school). Metrophobia often persists into adulthood, leading sufferers to avoid greeting cards, bookstores, coffee shops, and websites where poetry may lurk. They may even refuse to read unfamiliar books for fear of encountering an unexpected poem. Gaining a greater understanding of poetry is an important step in treating this unusual phobia, which seems to be just about as abstract as its subject matter.

THINGS TO AVOID: greeting cards; homework; English class; the film *Dead Poets Society*.

It seems there are very few metrophobes in the Middle East. One of the most popular television shows in the Persian Gulf region is *Million's Poet*, with over 70 million viewers—more than sports or the news. In a format similar to *American Idol*, amateur poets from across the region are judged on their poetry performances. The success of the show has also inspired a television channel dedicated completely to poetry.

||||| Statistics |||||

Dating to 2100 BC, the *Epic of Gilgamesh* is the oldest known poem, while the longest poem is the *Mahabharata*. It has more than 220,000 verses and around 1.8 million words. Anyone trying to overcome metrophobia by reading poetry should probably not start with that one.

Monophobia

MEANING: fear of being alone

ORIGIN: the Greek word *mono*, meaning "single" or "alone"

MONOPHOBIA is the fear of being alone. For some, solitude can be calming and rejuvenating, but for monophobes it's terrifying. Some with this phobia fear not just being alone in private, but also being alone in public. Monophobia may be related to a fear of the dark (nyctophobia) or a fear of being neglected. Sufferers fear that being alone leaves them at risk of robbery or attack, or that they might become sick or injured and never found. Commonly rooted in childhood fear of abandonment, this phobia tends to afflict people who lack confidence. Sufferers doubt their own judgment and ability to deal with emergency situations like injuries, burglaries, and home repair problems. Some fear being alone with their thoughts. Most monophobes avoid solitude, keeping as busy as possible with other people. When they do find themselves alone, they either stay in constant communication via phone or email, or create comforting background noise with television or music. Monophobia is the opposite of anthropophobia (the fear of people) and, while debilitating, is far easier to manage. For anthropophobes, there are 7.5 billion people to avoid; the monophobe just needs to find one of them.

THINGS TO AVOID: being single; the song "Monophobia" by Canadian producer Deadmau5.

‖‖ Phobia Trivia ‖‖

Monophobia is also known as autophobia, uniphobia, isolophobia, and eremophobia.

‖‖ Statistics ‖‖

About 1 in every 10 Americans lives alone.

Mycophobia

MEANING: fear of mushrooms

ORIGIN: the Latin word *myco*, meaning "fungus"

MYCOPHOBIA is the morbid fear of mushrooms, the root of which can be difficult to pinpoint. The most

common cause is fear of consuming a poisonous mushroom, resulting in illness or death. Most mycophobes avoid eating, smelling, touching, or even looking at mushrooms. An encounter with the fungus leads to crying, sweating, and an elevated body temperature and heart rate. Mycophobes might avoid the vegetable aisle at the grocery store, as well as restaurants that serve mushroom-based dishes. Cognitive therapy is a common treatment for reducing panic, anxiety, and malaise at the thought of the small, soft, white vegetables.

THINGS TO AVOID: open fields; the vegetable aisle; most restaurants and cafés; mushroom soup.

|||| Phobia Trivia ||||

Mycophobia is a branch of lachanophobia, the fear of vegetables. Known colloquially as a "magic" mushroom, a psilocybin mushroom is a fungus that contains various psychedelic compounds that produce an altered state of consciousness, as well as visual and auditory changes, when eaten. They have been used as drugs since ancient times, depicted in European and African rock art dating from the Stone Age. Despite being illegal in most countries, their recreational use is common.

|||| Statistics ||||

It is estimated that the fungus kingdom has up to 3.8 million species, 300 of which can be pathogenic to humans.

Myrmecophobia

MEANING: fear of ants

ORIGIN: the Greek word *myrmex*, meaning "ant"

MYRMECOPHOBIA is the intense fear of ants. The fear of ants has evolutionary roots: Early humans avoided creatures that could bite them or contaminate food. Being bitten by an ant as a child can cause myrmecophobia, particularly if an allergic reaction ensued. Myrmecophobes may fear large, hostile ants, but are just as likely to fear tiny, common black ants. The insects' militant organizational skills, ability to carry things many times their own weight, and occasional tendency to kill larger animals (and sometimes people) are sources of terror for myrmecophobes. Movies depicting colonies of killer ants swarming over their victims do little to allay fears. Sufferers avoid gardening and outdoor areas, especially in spring and summer when ants are rampant, and obsessively clean their homes and shut doors and windows to ward off intrusive ants. The thought of being dragged by killer ants to their queen to be devoured can cause tremors, vomiting, and fainting. In addition to counseling and medication, the primary method of treatment is gradual desensitization. A last resort is relocating to Antarctica, the only place on Earth where ants have not established vast and sophisticated colonies. Moving to the coastal regions of Australia is certainly not recommended (see Phobia Trivia on page 166).

THINGS TO AVOID: going outside; gardens or wooded areas; leaving food scraps around the house; some animal documentaries; the films *Antz*, *A Bug's Life,* and *Indiana Jones and the Kingdom of the Crystal Skull*; British singer Adam Ant; Australian coastal regions; Marvel superhero Ant-Man; the bulldog ant (do not, under any circumstances, search the internet for images of this ant).

Myrmecophobia belongs to the more general category entomophobia, the fear of insects. Ants evolved from wasp-like
ancestors around 140 million years ago. The bulldog ant holds
a place in *Guinness World Records* for the most dangerous
ant in the world. It is extremely aggressive and uses its sting
and jaw at the same time, injecting venom when it bites. With
three recorded human fatalities, it has killed adults within 15
minutes. It can be found in coastal regions of Australia.

|||| Statistics ||||

There are up to 22,000 species of ants worldwide that live in
colonies made up of millions of individuals.

Is for Nephophobia

Nephophobia

MEANING: fear of clouds

ORIGIN: the Greek word *nepho*, meaning "clouds"

NEPHOPHOBIA is the intense fear of clouds, including pictures or depictions of them. Clouds cause extreme anxiety in the sufferer, compelling them to stay inside on cloudy days or, in more extreme cases, move to climates with less cloud coverage, like Arizona or California. The fear may be caused by a bad experience with clouds or by a hereditary aversion to them. The association of clouds with bad weather, storms, damage, property destruction, and death contributes to nephophobia. Some nephophobes believe erroneously that a cloud can fall onto your head. In addition to anti-anxiety medication, the best remedy is learning about cloud behavior and that, outside of a very limited set of controlled conditions, a cloud cannot fall onto your head.

THINGS TO AVOID: the south coast of Alaska; the peak of Mount Kilimanjaro (as well as many other mountaintops); the United Kingdom and New Zealand (known by the Maori as "the land of the long white cloud"); plane travel; Joni Mitchell's song "Both Sides Now"; cloud nine.

|||| Phobia Trivia ||||

Nephophobia is closely related to homichlophobia (the fear of fog or humidity), nebulaphobia (the fear of fog and clouds), ombrophobia (the fear of rain), ceraunophobia (the fear of lightning and thunder), chionophobia (the fear of snow), and lilapsophobia (the fear of tornadoes and hurricanes). Some unlucky nephophobes find themselves afflicted with all these conditions, since clouds are involved in most other weather phenomena. San Francisco, in sunny California, averages 105 cloudy days per year.

There are 10 major cloud types: cirrus, stratus, cumulus, nimbus, cirrostratus, cirrocumulus, altostratus, altocumulus, stratocumulus, nimbostratus, and cumulonimbus.

Nomatophobia

MEANING: fear of names

ORIGIN: the Latin word *nam*, meaning "name"

NOMATOPHOBIA is the extreme fear of certain names or words, usually because of its special significance. Frequently the fear results from a painful experience: Getting bullied by a nasty boy named Glen, for example, might create a traumatic association of the name with the incident. The same thing can happen with other words: The word "ax" becomes a source of fear because of a tragic woodchopping incident. Nomatophobes refuse to say a particular name and dread the thought of hearing it. Even seeing the offending name in a book or newspaper triggers the sufferer. The condition can be so severe that the nomatophobe describes the word or name ("the brown-haired man") rather than saying it. While cognitive and behavioral therapy are often used to treat this condition, nomatophobes would do well to remember the famous children's rhyme, "sticks and stones may break my bones, but words will never hurt me." Maybe so, but that rhyme originates from the 19th century, when names like Glen, Justin, and Chad weren't nearly as common as they are today.

THINGS TO AVOID: people with scary names; television shows or films that have characters with scary names; books and newspapers that refer to people with scary names; baby name websites.

|||| Phobia Trivia ||||

Nomatophobia is a branch of logophobia (or verbophobia), which is the fear of words (from the Greek word *logos*, meaning "word").

|||| Statistics ||||

According to the Census Bureau, there are 151,671 different last names and 5,163 different first names in common use in the U.S. The most common name in America is John Smith—there are 47,596 of them.

Nomophobia

MEANING: fear of being without a cell phone

ORIGIN: a portmanteau of the words "no" and "mobile"

NOMOPHOBIA is the irrational fear of being without a cell phone, or finding oneself without phone signal or at low battery power. This phobia, which is a paradox of technology that is both freeing and enslaving, is brought about by an addiction to the device. Insecure people with low self-esteem who are constantly seeking reassurance often suffer from nomophobia, as do those who lack self-control and discipline. Naturally sociable extroverts who use their cell phones to excess can also suffer from this condition, as can those who've had a negative experience, such as having no cell phone signal during an emergency. Most nomophobes never switch off their phones and continually check their devices for signal, battery charge, and new messages or notifications. They keep their cell phones charging and within arm's reach, even while sleeping. Separation from one's phone causes extreme anxiety; most return home to retrieve a forgotten phone and avoid a full-fledged panic attack. This obsession interferes with a sufferer's personal relationships, as well as affects their work life. Treatments include relaxation techniques such as yoga and positive visualization, as well as psychotherapy, hypnotherapy, and, in extreme cases, medication. Systematic desensitization starts with a few phone-free minutes before working up to venturing from home entirely without a phone (something that even non-nomophobes might consider an achievement).

THINGS TO AVOID: not charging your cell phone properly; forgetting your cell phone; remote places with no phone coverage; cheap and limited phone plans.

||||| Phobia Trivia |||||

The term nomophobia was coined by YouGov, a U.K. research organization that found in a 2008 study that 53 percent of cell phone users felt anxious when they were unable to use their phones, and over half never shut their phones off. A 2012 study at South Africa's Tshwane University of Technology found that college students spent up to nine hours every day on their phones and that cell phones are "possibly the biggest non-drug addiction of the 21st century." A 2016 study of South Korean students published in the journal *Science Direct* found that 25 percent were addicted to their smartphones.

Almost 5 billion people in the world have cell phones—that's two-thirds of the world's population. Almost 75 percent of Americans are smartphone users, but the number of nomophobes is not yet known.

Nyctophobia

MEANING: fear of darkness

ORIGIN: the Greek word *nyktos*, meaning "night"

NYCTOPHOBIA is the intense fear of the dark, not usually the darkness itself, but of the possible dangers that the darkness conceals. While fear of the dark is quite natural, nyctophobia arises from an experience like getting scared by a noise in the dark or seeing a horror film depicting terrifying acts during the hours of darkness. Many nyctophobes fear the dark because of the unknown. They fear that monsters or ghosts are lurking out of sight, waiting to attack, or that they will be swallowed alive by the dark. Darkness can cause dizziness, trembling, and a shortness of breath. Few afflicted with nyctophobia choose to talk about their condition for fear of ridicule. Sufferers avoid dark places and being out after dark, leave lights on all night, seldom sleep alone, stay awake all night, and check and recheck under the bed and in the closet for bogeymen, ghosts, monsters, or intruders. This can lead to extreme sleep deprivation, affecting their work and personal life. Sleep deprivation can also result in hallucinations, leading the nyctophobe to believe they've actually seen bogeymen, ghosts, monsters, or intruders, exacerbating their fears.

THINGS TO AVOID: nighttime; camping; the opening line of Simon & Garfunkel's song "The Sound of Silence"; power outages.

Phobia Trivia

Nyctophobia is also known as achluophobia, lygophobia, or scotophobia. Actors Keanu Reeves and Megan Fox are afraid of the dark, as is Jennifer Love Hewitt, who also fears monsters under the bed.

Statistics

In parts of Norway, 200 miles north of the Arctic Circle, there is complete darkness for three months at a time—not ideal for nyctophobes, but a good place to vacation in summer, when the sun never sets.

Is for
Omphalophobia

Odynophobia

MEANING: fear of pain

ORIGIN: the Greek word *odyn*, meaning "pain"

ODYNOPHOBIA is the fear of pain. While very few people are in favor of pain, odynophobes are petrified of it. Odynophobia is more common in the elderly, who have witnessed friends suffering pain or regularly experience pain themselves. Highly emotionally sensitive people are also more likely to suffer from this condition: Their empathy for other people's pain increases their fear of experiencing it themselves. Having suffered extreme pain in the past can also give rise to this phobia. As pain can cause fear, and the distress of fear can cause pain, odynophobia turns into a vicious cycle. Sufferers of this condition experience extreme anxiety at even the thought of pain, frequently leading to excessive use of pain relievers that can result in addiction or overdose. Odynophobia is treated with meditation, relaxation techniques, or support groups. If none of that works, you could try embracing pain by becoming a sadomasochist, or developing the genetic abnormality that causes CIPA (see Phobia Trivia). If all else fails, try watching the scene from *Rocky IV* when Rocky, presumably in extreme pain, is repeatedly told by his trainer Duke to feel "No pain! No pain!" That seemed to work pretty well.

THINGS TO AVOID: contact sports; the aging process; day-to-day mishaps like falling down a flight of stairs.

||||| Phobia Trivia |||||

Odynophobia is also known as odynephobia, agliophobia, or algophobia (from the Greek word *algos*, also meaning "pain").

Caused by a genetic mutation that prevents the formation of nerve cells that are responsible for transmitting signals of pain, congenital insensitivity to pain with anhidrosis (CIPA) is an extremely rare disorder that prevents the sensation of pain, ideal if you're an odynophobe.

||||| Statistics |||||

There are at least 28 known scales that are used to measure pain. One of them is the Numeric Rating Scale (NRS-11), an 11-point scale, with 0 being no pain, 1 to 3 being mild pain, 4 to 6 being moderate pain, and 7 to 10 being severe pain.

Omphalophobia

MEANING: fear of belly buttons

ORIGIN: the Greek word *omphalo*, meaning "navel"

Not to be confused with koumpounophobia (the fear of buttons), OMPHALOPHOBIA is the fear of belly buttons. One of the least documented phobias, it affects men and women equally. Omphalophobes fear both their own navel and those of other people. Sufferers may be afraid to touch their navel and do not like others touching it. They shun the thought of touching someone else's navel; the mere sight of a navel is enough to disgust some subjects. Symptoms include trembling, nausea, vomiting, panic, and fleeing the sight of an exposed navel. The fear is widely thought to be linked to the belly button's association with the umbilical cord and womb; some sufferers fear that part of the umbilical cord has been left behind in their navel. Young sufferers may worry that the contents of their stomach can spill out of their belly buttons, or that it is dirty. Many omphalophobes begin early life with a fascination with their belly button, regularly poking at it until pain results, bringing on the phobia. Anxiety associated with omphalophobia can affect relationships and productivity. While it is a very treatable phobia, many people refuse to seek help for some reason.

THINGS TO AVOID: beaches and swimming pools; the swimsuit category of beauty pageants; Olympic events like swimming, diving, and beach volleyball; pornography; pregnant women with protruding navels. Unclothed Ken and Barbie dolls, as well as most mannequins, are generally navel-free and considered safe.

|||| Phobia Trivia ||||

Famous omphalophobes include English singer Jenny Frost and Khloe Kardashian.

|||| Statistics ||||

The average man has 1.8 milligrams of belly button lint at any given time. Who knows how much a blue whale has—they have belly buttons 8 inches wide.

Oneirogmophobia

MEANING: fear of wet dreams

ORIGIN: the Greek word *oneiro*, meaning "dream"

ONEIROGMOPHOBIA is the persistent and compulsive fear of wet dreams. While typically suffered by adolescent men in early puberty, the condition can affect people of any age. Wet dreams occur without any manual stimulation, a result of raging hormones, and usually cannot be controlled. It is this feeling of a loss of control that causes the phobia. Feelings of guilt and shame, especially for people from a strong religious background that discourages sexual urges, may also contribute to the condition. The surprise of waking up with wet bed sheets can result in panic and a desire to flee, which can be awkward when wearing wet pajamas. Because nocturnal emissions are a natural phenomenon, medications are not prescribed. Treatment includes sex education and assurance that there is nothing to feel ashamed about.

THINGS TO AVOID: erotic or arousing television shows and movies, particularly just before bed; sexy books and magazines; silky bedclothes.

||||| Phobia Trivia |||||

The medical term for a wet dream is a "nocturnal emission."

||||| Statistics |||||

It varies, but some studies suggest that, in the United States, 83 percent of men experience a wet dream at some time in their life. In Indonesia, 97 percent of men have had one by the age of 24.

Optophobia

MEANING: fear of opening one's eyes

ORIGIN: the Latin word *opt*, meaning "eyes"

OPTOPHOBIA is the fear of opening one's eyes. An actual phobia, optophobia is caused by witnessing a traumatic event, like a fatal accident or a partner's infidelity. Sufferers refuse to open their eyes for fear of seeing something that will cause displeasure or fear. Optophobia can be situational, arising while watching a horror movie or monster truck rally. The thought of opening one's eyes in scary circumstances can lead to heart palpitations, vomiting, and panic attacks. Treatment involves hypnotherapy and anti-anxiety medication. In extreme cases, the optophobe becomes isolated and may not leave the house, preferring to stay indoors in a dimly lit room, watching (or perhaps just listening to) their favorite movie—*Eyes Wide Shut.*

THINGS TO AVOID: opening your eyes; getting out of bed; leaving the house.

|||| Phobia Trivia ||||

The World Health Organization estimates there are 39 million blind people in the world. While there are no estimates on how many people keep their eyes shut voluntarily, optophobia is a rare condition, and the number is likely much closer to 39.

|||| Statistics ||||

According to RecordSetter, Michael Thomas of Florida holds the record for the longest time without blinking. In 2015, he managed to keep his eyes open for one hour and 5.61 seconds.

Is for Pogonophobia

Panophobia

MEANING: fear of everything

ORIGIN: the Greek word *pan*, meaning "all"

PANOPHOBIA is the fear of everything. Sufferers worry excessively that terrible things will happen to them. Negative news or trauma cause the onset of this phobia; it can also be triggered by other phobias. The panophobe fears anxiety itself, creating a vicious circle and self-fulfilling prophecy with intensifying symptoms. Living in a constant state of fear, panophobes believe that evil is lurking everywhere, just waiting to befall them. Panophobia leads to social withdrawal and isolation as the sufferer seeks to avoid cats, wind, flutes, ants, people, and the many, many other phobia-inducing sources. While relaxation techniques like yoga, tai chi, and meditation are used to treat this condition, treatment becomes counterproductive when the panophobe's fears include yoga, tai chi, and meditation. Sufferers sometimes can't remember how their innumerable fears began in the first place, leading to paranoia and making life even harder (and scarier).

THINGS TO AVOID: everything; existing; waking the Greek god Pan from an afternoon nap (see Phobia Trivia below); talking to Woody Allen, who has a fear of almost everything; the Michael Bublé song "Everything."

||||| Phobia Trivia |||||

Panophobia is also known as panphobia, omniphobia, and pantophobia. The word "panophobia" originated from Pan in Greek mythology, the god of the wild who was part goat, part man. When disturbed from his afternoon naps, Pan shouted angrily, giving rise to the word "panic." Woody Allen is generally considered to be a panophobe, afraid of practically everything, including heights, insects, bright colors, dogs, deer, small rooms, enclosed spaces, elevators, sunshine, crowds, cancer, and sources of evil.

||||| Statistics |||||

The Michael Bublé song "Everything," released in 2007, reached number 31 in the U.S. Billboard charts.

Papaphobia

MEANING: fear of the pope

ORIGIN: the Latin word *papa*, meaning "pope"

PAPAPHOBIA is the intense fear or dread of the pope. For millions, the pope is a beloved spiritual leader, believed to be the successor to St. Peter, who was given the keys to heaven by Jesus. Papaphobes, however, experience excessive sweating, rapid breathing, and extreme anxiety at the sight of the head of the Catholic church. The condition usually involves opposition to the Roman Catholic Church, but can also stem from a dislike of authority. The pope's white cassock and huge crown-like headdress instills terror in young papaphobes, which sometimes persists into adulthood. While the thought or mention of the pope may be enough to elicit symptoms in the sufferer, it is predominantly the sight of the Holy Pontiff that instills genuine fear. Fortunately this condition doesn't affect the day-to-day lives of papaphobes who don't live in or near the Vatican, as the pope rarely leaves.

THINGS TO AVOID: Rome and the Vatican; golf carts and other vehicles that resemble the popemobile; Catholic churches; papal dictates; TV shows like *The Young Pope*, *The Borgias*, and *Animal Kingdom*.

Papaphobia is related to a number of other phobias: hierophobia (the fear of holy people or sacred things), ecclesiophobia (the fear of church, organized religion, or holy people), and hagiophobia (the fear of saints or holy things).

There have been 266 popes throughout history, which seems like a lot for the papaphobe to avoid, but only two are still alive. Both live in the Vatican, making papaphobia a lot more manageable.

Papyrophobia

MEANING: fear of paper

ORIGIN: the Greek word *papyro*, meaning "paper"

PAPYROPHOBIA is the persistent fear of paper. This phobia is usually rooted in a paper-related experience, like getting pelted with a tightly crumpled ball of paper or a particularly bad papercut. It can also be genetic, but in many cases psychologists are unable to pinpoint the cause of this rare phobia. Encountered with paper, papyrophobes scream, cry, sweat, panic, or feel a sense of impending disaster, all of which can lead to ridicule from peers. Papyrophobes fear all sorts of paper, from plain sheets and crumpled balls to gift wrap, origami paper, and paper bags. Intensity of fear varies based on paper size: A poster is likely to cause more anxiety than a Post-it Note. Touching paper, writing on it, looking at it, using it, or tearing it elicits an adverse reaction, making it extremely difficult to hold down a job or exist comfortably on a daily basis (or go to the bathroom). Psychiatric counseling and group therapy are the most common treatments. Teaching sufferers that paper poses little threat, apart from papercuts, also helps.

THINGS TO AVOID: school; newspapers; books; magazines; wrapped presents; the bathroom; having a cold.

|||| Phobia Trivia ||||

American actress Megan Fox has papyrophobia, particularly the sound of paper tearing and erasers on paper.

|||| Statistics ||||

There is a common myth that you can't fold a single sheet of paper in half more than seven times, which is true for a standard size sheet of printer paper. However, if you change the size or thickness of the paper, you can increase the number of possible folds.

Pediophobia

MEANING: fear of dolls

ORIGIN: the Greek word *paidion*, meaning "little child"

PEDIOPHOBIA is the fear dolls. Long a source of entertainment for children, dolls are a cause for terror for some people, who run away at the sight of the harmless toys. Believed to be a type of automatonophobia (the fear of humanoid figures, like mannequins, dummies, robotic figures, and wax models), pediophobia is relatively common and can include fear of all stuffed toys and dolls, particularly old-fashioned china dolls and those that talk or move. The phobia may stem from an association of dolls with witchcraft (such as voodoo dolls), leading to the belief that dolls are evil. The familiar, human-like appearance of a doll mixed with its inanimate characteristics (like lack of breathing, coldness, and absent stare) can produce an eerie quality that triggers revulsion in some people, especially children who can't separate fantasy from reality. Pop culture has also done little to ameliorate the fear of dolls: A number of movies depict dolls as deadly sentient beings bent on destruction. The mere sight of a doll can elicit screaming, crying, a sense of impending danger, and an overwhelming desire to get away. Exposure therapy, where the patient eventually grows accustomed to dolls with gradual exposure, is a common treatment. Just be sure to ignore those vacant eyes that somehow follow you around the room.

THINGS TO AVOID: the 1988 film *Child's Play*; puppet shows; dollhouses; young girls; the 1996 *Seinfeld* episode "The Doll."

|||| Phobia Trivia ||||

Many adult sufferers of pediopobia are also known to fear little children, likening the diminutive size of the children to that of dolls.

Dolls have been a part of human culture for over 4,000 years, originally made of clay, stone, wood, bone, and ivory.

Peladophobia

MEANING: fear of bald people

ORIGIN: the Spanish word *pelado*, meaning "bald"

PELADOPHOBIA is the excessive fear of bald people, which affects men and women of all ages. Sometimes the result of a genetic predisposition (much like balding), this phobia can also originate from an unpleasant experience with a bald person. With symptoms like shaking, shortness of breath, and feelings of dread at the sight of a folically challenged person, peladophobes go to extreme lengths to stay away from them, going so far as to avoid Mr. Clean products. While some sufferers take medication to treat the condition, the most common form of treatment is exposure therapy, presumably involving bald men parading past the peladophobe until the hairless volunteers are no longer a source of distress (or until the sufferer goes mad, whichever comes first). In extreme cases, it's best to just avoid baldness at both ends of the age spectrum: old-age homes and hospital maternity wards.

THINGS TO AVOID: Telly Savalas movies and television shows, most notably *Kojak*; overzealous barber shops; men over 50; Florida.

Peladophobia is related to phalacrophobia, which is the fear of becoming bald.

About 85 percent of men over 50 will have experienced a significant amount of hair loss.

Pentheraphobia

MEANING: fear of mothers-in-law

ORIGIN: the Greek word *penthera*, meaning "mother-in-law"

While most people's feelings about their spouse's mom fall in a range between grudging warmth to barely concealed hatred, those with PENTHERAPHOBIA actually fear their mothers-in-law. The phobia is surprisingly common, although frequently unspoken, and is often intensified in the case of a particularly overbearing mother-in-law. The fear can derive from the disheartening realization that your mother-in-law doesn't live up to expectations based on your own mother. The condition is exacerbated when a mother-in-law is highly opinionated or too hands-on in her child's life. Women with domineering personalities can be intimidating to their in-laws, triggering the phobia. Pop culture and the numerous clichés about harridan mothers-in-law can worsen the condition, which causes nausea, sweating, trembling, irregular heartbeat, fainting, dread, and panic. Pentheraphobia is sometimes cured by an open discussion with the offending mother-in-law to set boundaries and clear the air, while medication or therapy can also be helpful. But of all the available remedies, the quickest and most popular is divorce.

THINGS TO AVOID: family gatherings; living with or near your in-laws; talking about your mother-in-law; looking at pictures of your mother-in-law; thinking about your mother-in-law.

‖‖ Phobia Trivia ‖‖

The sansevieria plant is commonly known as mother-in-law's tongue because of its long, sharp, spiky leaves. Related phobias are vitricophobia (the fear of step-fathers), novercaphobia (the fear of step-mothers), and soceraphobia (the fear of parents-in-law).

‖‖ Statistics ‖‖

According to a 2009 study conducted by Terri Apter, a psychologist at Cambridge University, more than 60 percent of women felt their mother-in-law had caused them long-term stress, compared with only 15 percent of men.

Phasmophobia

MEANING: fear of ghosts

ORIGIN: the Greek word *phasmos*, meaning "phantom" or "supernatural being"

PHASMOPHOBIA is the morbid fear of ghosts, which affects people of all ages. The fear of ghosts is ingrained in many cultures and religions, and phobias are fueled by superstitions, television shows, and films perpetuating the notion of ghosts as malevolent and vengeful beings. Ghosts are regarded as omens of death or bad tidings, and some scientists believe phasmophobia is actually a fear of our own death. Symptoms include heart palpitations, hallucinations, and bed-wetting, even in children. Insomnia is a common side effect, which can lead to mood swings, nervousness, and impaired performance at school or work. Many sufferers refuse to sleep in the dark or alone. Halloween is an especially stressful time of year. Children suffering from phasmophobia should be assured by their parents that ghosts aren't real and that there is nothing to fear. In cases where the parents themselves have phasmophobia, the only realistic option is to call Ghostbusters.

THINGS TO AVOID: Halloween; the movie *Ghost*; spooky amusement park rides and attractions; *Scooby-Doo*; books written by ghostwriters; Johnny Cash's song "Ghost Riders in the Sky"; *Casper the Friendly Ghost* (despite his alleged demeanor); the movie *Ghostbusters* (as well as its sequel, its remake, and its theme song), despite the main characters' good intentions.

|||| Phobia Trivia ||||

Phasmophobia is also known as spectrophobia; "specter" is another term for a ghost that originates from "reflection" (spectrophobia is specifically the fear of one's own reflection). Phasmophobia is often accompanied by nyctophobia, which is the fear of darkness (where ghosts are most likely to strike). Many phasmophobes also suffer from pneumatiphobia (the fear of spirits), demonophobia (the fear of demons), satanophobia (the fear of Satan or devils), hadephobia or stygiophobia (the fear of hell), wiccaphobia (the fear of witches), or bogyphobia (the fear of the bogeyman). Shaggy and Scooby from *Scooby-Doo* are renowned phasmophobes, as are the Wari, an Amazonian rainforest tribe. The Wari believe that spirits of dead people appear as "jima," who grab victims with their strong, cold, poisonous hands, trying to pull the person's spirit away.

||||| Statistics |||||

A 2018 study of 2,000 Americans found that 60 percent claim to have seen a ghost at some time in their lives.

Philemaphobia

MEANING: fear of kissing

ORIGIN: the Greek word *philema*, meaning "kissing"

Also spelled "philematophobia," PHILEMAPHOBIA is the extreme fear of kissing. While kissing is a natural expression of affection for many people, some are petrified of it. Philemaphobia may be rooted in cultural or religious beliefs that kissing is sinful, or it can arise from a history of sexual abuse. Failed relationships can also lead to the association of kissing with unwanted emotional involvement. Those who feel violated by touch can also be afraid of kissing, as can those who fear intimacy and vulnerability. Concern over bad breath or bodily odors, especially for those who also suffer from bromidrophobia (the fear of bodily odors), can turn a simple kiss into an act of terror. Fear of germs or illness—such as herpes and mononucleosis, known as the "kissing disease"—may also contribute to a fear of kissing. Symptoms like profuse sweating, trembling, weeping, and losing consciousness are neither conducive to kissing nor are they to satisfying personal relationships or social interactions. The most common basis for philemaphobia is the sufferer's fear of not measuring up to their partner's expectations, particularly in young and inexperienced kissers. Treatment may involve counseling, but exposure therapy is usually the most successful method. As they say, practice makes perfect.

THINGS TO AVOID: soap operas and many other television shows; rom-coms; kissing booths; the 2018 film *The Kissing Booth*; greetings at family gatherings, in particular long-unseen aunts; rock band KISS; Elvis Presley's song "Kissing Cousins"; Ed Sheeran's song "Kiss Me"; countless others songs about kissing.

Phobia Trivia

Related to philemaphobia are malaxophobia and sarmassophobia, each the fear of love play. Philemaphobia is rife in conservative countries. In India, kissing in public used to be a criminal offense and, as recently as 2007, two people in Dubai, United Arab Emirates, were fined and jailed for a month for kissing in public.

Statistics

Kissing is a complex behavior that requires significant muscular coordination, involving a total of 34 facial muscles and 112 postural muscles (assuming the standing position).

Philophobia

MEANING: fear of falling in love

ORIGIN: the Greek word *filos*, meaning "loving" or "beloved"

PHILOPHOBIA is the irrational fear of falling in love or emotional attachment. Love is one of the most beautiful and amazing parts of life, but it can also be frightening, and for philophobes, downright terrifying. Fear of abandonment is typically at the root of this condition. Someone who was abandoned as a child, is the child of divorced parents, has survived physical or emotional abuse, or has endured a painful breakup is more likely to develop a fear of love, averse to the risks involved with commitment and vulnerability. Or the phobia may be based in culture or religion: Sufferers from strict or repressive societies may come to fear persecution or incurring the wrath of God. Philophobes fear romantic love and emotional bonds, avoid close relationships, often live alone, skip social gatherings, and avoid long conversations for fear of falling in love. They also avoid other people in relationships, as just seeing people in love causes dizziness, nausea, and panic. Attending a wedding is tantamount to torture for the extreme sufferer. Support groups encourage philophobes to open up about their fears, and a number of online forums can teach victims that the benefits of love outweigh the costs. The more successful of these websites should consider diversifying into online dating.

THINGS TO AVOID: social events and interactions; weddings; rom-coms.

||||| Phobia Trivia |||||

It is believed that England's Queen Elizabeth I, who never married, was a philophobe. Her condition may have arisen from the fact that her mother, Anne Boleyn, was executed by order of her father King Henry VIII. She can probably be forgiven for believing that romantic relationships end in tragedy.

||||| Statistics |||||

Philophobia is more common in women than in men, and statistics suggest that as many as 250,000 Americans suffer from it.

Phobophobia

MEANING: fear of phobias

ORIGIN: the Greek word *phobo*, meaning "irrational fear"

PHOBOPHOBIA is the fear of phobias. Sufferers are overwhelmed at the thought of developing an irrational fear, suffering a panic, and the attendant embarrassment. Some people with phobophobia have other phobias and are afraid of developing more; phobophobes who are otherwise phobia-free fear developing any other phobias (and if that sentence isn't enough to scare the average phobophobe, not much will). The fear itself can lead to a self-perpetuating cycle, resulting in escalating circular fears. Phobophobia is different from other phobias in that there is no environmental stimulus to trigger it, but rather internal dread over contracting a yet-to-be-determined phobia. Sufferers curtail their daily activities for risk of encountering something they might find themselves scared of and, in anticipation of fear, experience uncontrollable sweating, trembling, screaming, and an intense desire to flee. The problem is that they have no idea what they're trying to flee from, making it a somewhat futile reaction. Treatment may include behavioral therapy and hypnosis, but the nebulous nature of this condition makes it difficult to treat. Many people view phobophobia as a delusional condition with no scientific basis, but sufferers can take solace in the fact that one of America's great leaders, Franklin D. Roosevelt, acknowledged its existence when he said, "The only thing we have to fear is fear itself."

THINGS TO AVOID: anything that you find really scary that might lead to a phobia; this book; FDR's inaugural address.

|||| Phobia Trivia ||||

Phobophobia is related to panophobia, panphobia, pantophobia, and pamphobia (which are all the fear of everything), as well as polyphobia (which is the fear of many things).

|||| Statistics ||||

An estimated 9.1 percent of Americans, more than 19 million people, have some kind of phobia or phobias.

Phronemophobia

MEANING: fear of thinking

ORIGIN: the Greek word *phron*, meaning "thinking"

While some people prefer to be left alone with their thoughts, PHRONEMOPHOBIA is the extreme fear of thinking. Unwanted, intrusive thoughts that enter the mind involuntarily may cause the sufferer to fear that thoughts will turn into actions and something dire will occur. For example, a phronemophobe may worry that thoughts about murder will lead to the act itself. Traumatic memories are another source of fear, making the sufferer afraid to think of anything at all. The trouble is that it is terribly hard, if not impossible, to avoid thinking. A common treatment method is talk therapy to clarify the difference between fantasy and reality and help the patient recognize that what happens in the mind does not necessarily happen in real life. Keeping busy is another way to keep negative thoughts at bay. To combat the neverending barrage of unwanted thoughts, phronemophobes typically keep themselves distracted, avoid being alone, and stay as active as possible, doing anything to stop idle thoughts from turning into…the unthinkable.

THINGS TO AVOID: education and study; being awake; being asleep; life in general; the sculpture The Thinker by Auguste Rodin.

|||| Phobia Trivia ||||

Phronemophobia often goes hand in hand with mnemophobia, which is the fear of memories.

The Thinker is a bronze sculpture by Auguste Rodin; 700,000 people view it in Paris each year.

Pinaciphobia

MEANING: fear of lists

ORIGIN: the Greek word *pinaci*, meaning "list"

PINACIPHOBIA is the intense fear of lists or anything in list format, like directories, inventories, and catalogs. A traumatic list-related experience, such as losing an important list or forgetting something essential because you didn't make a list, is the most common cause of this phobia. Sufferers might also fear a lengthy to-do list, daunted by the thought of being unable to achieve everything on it, leading to disappointment or reprimand. Those who detest order or resent authority may also find lists burdensome. This disorder can severely hinder a person's daily life. The mere sight of a list causes anxiety; a list of things to do incites feelings of being trapped and out of control, possibly leading to a panic attack. While checking completed items off a list is enjoyable and satisfying for most people, it is anything but for the pinaciphobe.

THINGS TO AVOID: directories; inventories; catalogs; phonebooks; grocery shopping (unless you have a good memory).

|||| Phobia Trivia ||||

The fear of lists is also known as katastichophobia. And the more specific fear of phobia lists is phopinaciphobia.

Experts believe that you can hold seven items in short-term memory for only 20 to 30 seconds at a time. So if you suffer from pinaciphobia, you might find yourself making a lot of trips to the grocery store.

Pogonophobia

MEANING: fear of beards

ORIGIN: the Greek word *pogon*, meaning "beard"

POGONOPHOBIA is the irrational and persistent fear of beards or people with beards, known to affect thousands of people around the world. While beards are often viewed as a symbol of manliness or ruggedness, they may also be associated with illness and homelessness; fear may develop because of a perceived lack of hygiene related to beards. Stereotypes about bearded men being untrustworthy, or "hiding" behind a beard, can also lead to the phobia. While fear of beards affects people of all ages and genders, it is far more common in women. Psychotherapy has been one of the most successful techniques in treating pogonophobia. Pogonophobia is principally directed at men with beards. Statistics for the fear of women with beards are harder to come by (and you don't have to be a pogonophobe to be afraid of them—that's just plain scary for everybody).

THINGS TO AVOID: Key West's annual Ernest Hemingway Look-Alike Contest; Kenny Rogers; Santa; malls at Christmastime.

There has not been a bearded president in the U.S. since the 1800s. These days, politicians find the clean-shaven look is better for instilling trust in the minds of the voters and avoiding unnecessary suspicion. Beardism (discrimination on the basis of facial hair) is a real historical phenomenon. It was only in 2012 that Disneyland lifted its ban on employee beards, a policy that lasted for nearly 60 years. Clearly there was a pogonophobe among Disney's executives in the 1950s. Pogonophobia is the opposite of pogonophilia, which is the love of beards or bearded people.

In a 2018 survey conducted by Wahl Clipper Corporation, Philadelphia took the title as America's number-one Most Facial Hair–Friendly City. Chicago was second, and Atlanta third.

Pteronophobia

MEANING: fear of being tickled by feathers

ORIGIN: the Greek word *ptero*, meaning "wing" or "feather"

PTERONOPHOBIA is the intense fear of being tickled by feathers. While some love to be tickled, enjoying the laughter and release of endorphins, pteronophobes fear it, especially if a dreaded feather is involved. This phobia is common in people with an exaggerated bodily response to tickling. An irrational under-standing of the concept of "being tickled to death" can also lead to pteronophobia. A traumatic experience of being pinned down and tickled involuntarily can also lead to the phobia, especially if a feather was used. Pteronophobes are often introverted and usually avoid bodily contact with other people. Just seeing a feather results in nausea and panic. While relaxation techniques have had some success in treating pteronophobia, if that doesn't work, all you have to do is avoid human contact and be alone for the rest of your life, because you can't tickle yourself (unless you're a schizophrenic, in which case you've got bigger things to worry about).

THINGS TO AVOID: feathers; aviaries; chicken coops; feather dusters; writing implements from the days of yore; feather pil-lows and cushions; people who are prone to tickling.

||||| Phobia Trivia |||||

Philosophers going back to Aristotle pondered the question of why we're unable to tickle ourselves. Scientists believe that when we are tickled our bodies panic and go into a state of self-defense. This response comes from our early ancestors' reaction to predators (such as a spider crawling on the body). Today, because we know there is no danger, our reaction to tickling is to laugh. This occurs either because we are taken by surprise or in anticipation of being tickled. When we try to tickle ourselves, there is no such reaction—we're not quick enough to fool ourselves. Some schizophrenics, however, who have difficulty distinguishing self-generated from external touch, are able to tickle themselves.

The emperor penguin is believed to have the most plumage of any bird, having up to 80,000 individual feathers.

Pugophobia

MEANING: fear of buttocks

ORIGIN: the Greek word *puge*, meaning "buttock"

PUGOPHOBIA is the irrational fear of buttocks. This phobia is commonly suffered by young children, triggered by painful experiences excreting large feces, and can then persist into adulthood. People who are forced to sit all day, including the elderly and those with disabilities, can also develop pugophobia. Extreme sufferers refuse to sit on their buttocks, which can lead to kathisophobia (the fear of sitting). The thought or sight of buttocks, their own or the buttocks of others, is enough to instill intense fear in pugophobes, many of whom avoid viewing that area of the anatomy. They refuse to look in the mirror while naked, and avoid areas like locker rooms and nude beaches, where buttocks are likely to be on display. Even clothed buttocks can be a source of consternation for some pugophobes, as can the Sir Mix-a-Lot song "Baby Got Back."

THINGS TO AVOID: nude beaches; gyms and locker rooms; Greek and Roman statues; Kim Kardashian; the Sir Mix-a-Lot song "Baby Got Back"; the *Friends* episode "The One with Ross's Inappropriate Song."

|||| Phobia Trivia ||||

The gluteus maximus (aka the buttocks) is the largest muscle in the human body. It is also one of the most erogenous areas for evolutionary reasons. In women, round and voluptuous buttocks are the result of an abundance of the female hormone estrogen, indicating youth and fertility to potential mates. In men, muscular buttocks indicate a strong thrusting ability, making him more adept at mating and reproduction. Related to pugophobia is rectophobia, which is the fear of the rectum.

|||| Statistics ||||

The record-holder for world's biggest butt is Mikel Ruffinelli, a Los Angeles psychology student. Her hips measure over 8 feet in circumference.

Is for
Quadraphobia

Quadraphobia

MEANING: fear of the number four

ORIGIN: the Latin word *quattuor*, meaning "four"

QUADRAPHOBIA is the unreasonable fear of the number four or things that come in fours. Superstition surrounding the number is common in Asia, similar to the Western fear of the number 13 (triskaidekaphobia). Pronounced "pin-yin" in Chinese, the word for "four" sounds similar to the word for "death" or "disease," and because of this is considered extremely unlucky. Fear of the number 4 permeates all facets of life in China (and, to a lesser extent, Korea, Vietnam, and Japan). Addresses and license plates don't contain the number, especially not as the last digit. Some buildings don't have a fourth floor, or any floor with a four in it. Military aircraft and ships avoid the number four, and weddings often don't include a table four. Hospitals are particularly averse to the number, and you'll be hard pushed finding four in any health facility. April 4 is considered an exceptionally unlucky day, and people avoid phone numbers, home addresses, and ID numbers with four. When Beijing lost its bid to host the 2000 Olympic Games, it was speculated that they then held off until 2008 before bidding again, so as to avoid the 2004 Olympics. In Cantonese-speaking regions, 14 and 24 are considered even more unlucky. The word for 14 sounds like "will certainly die," and 24 like "easy to die." In Mandarin-speaking regions, 14 sounds like "wants to" or "is going to die," while 74 sounds like "will certainly die," or "will die in anger."

THINGS TO AVOID: TV channels with four in them; fourth floors of buildings; flight numbers with four in them; the fourth day of the month, every day in April, and years that have four in them.

Quadraphobia is a subclass of numerophobia (the fear of numbers) and is also known as tetraphobia (from the Greek word *tetra*, meaning "four"). Similar phobias include quattuor-decimphobia (the fear of the number 14), quadragintaphobia (the fear of the number 40), and quadricentumphobia (the fear of the number 400).

||| | **Statistics** ||| |

A 2001 study reported in the *British Medical Journal* found that Asians were 13 percent more likely to die of heart failure on the fourth day of the month, and in California, Asians were 27 percent more likely to die of a heart attack on that day. The purpose of the study was to see if superstitious stress could lead to physical maladies.

Is for Rhytiphobia

Rhabdophobia

MEANING: fear of magic

ORIGIN: the Greek word *rhabdo*, meaning "stick," "rod," or "switch"

RHABDOPHOBIA is the intense fear of magic, literally the fear of a magic wand. Caused by a childhood encounter with a creepy magician or magic trick gone wrong, it can also be an inherited condition. Rhabdophobes are fearful of magicians, illusionists, and spell casters, and go to extreme lengths to avoid magic shows and kids' birthday parties. Witnessing a sleight of hand can result in dizziness, accelerated heart rate, or a feeling of being choked. Talk therapy and relaxation techniques are prescribed to those who are overwhelmed by their fears. Exposure therapy may also help.

THINGS TO AVOID: magicians; illusionists; kids' birthday parties; circuses; the Bruno Mars album *24K Magic*; the Orlando Magic basketball team; the 1978 American horror film *Magic*; the 2013 Indonesian soap opera *Magic*; the 1917 silent Hungarian drama *Magic*; the Harry Potter books and films.

|||| Phobia Trivia ||||

Magic has been used as a form of entertainment since the ancient Greeks. Stone Age cave paintings also show figures holding sticks, which may have represented a form of magic wand. The magic-related expression "sleight of hand" is often erroneously written as "slight of hand." "Sleight," however, is the correct word, from the Old Norse word *slaegr*, meaning "sly."

Statistics

The value of the Harry Potter franchise is estimated at $25 billion. The books alone have sold more than 500 million copies, making them the best-selling book series in history. Instead of "sex sells," perhaps the saying should be changed to "magic sells."

Rhytiphobia

MEANING: fear of getting wrinkles

ORIGIN: the Greek word *rhyti*, meaning "wrinkle"

RHYTIPHOBIA is the fear of wrinkles or becoming wrinkled. To some, wrinkles represent wisdom or having led a happy life. Rhytiphobes, however, find them terrifying, fearing that wrinkles will make them ugly or expose their actual age. Sufferers of this phobia tend to have low self-esteem and be exceptionally vain. They often avoid elderly people and, in more extreme cases, resort to cosmetic surgery to remove wrinkles and appear more youthful. Others adopt a flat affect, suppressing smiles and laughter in an attempt to prevent wrinkles. Therapy is the most common treatment, with the goal of basing self-worth on inner beauty rather than physical beauty, but in many cases the sufferer has difficulty grappling with the fact that "time waits for no man."

THINGS TO AVOID: the passage of time; Gordon Ramsay; retirement facilities and nursing homes; Florida; the 46 million Americans over 65 years old.

Many celebrities have at least a mild case of rhytiphobia; Kim Kardashian is an acute sufferer. She doesn't smile or laugh for fear of aging. In the caption of an unusually smiley Instagram post she wrote, "See I do smile…even laugh on occasion. Not too often though because it causes wrinkles."

The global antiaging market is worth more than $250 billion.

Is for
Sinistrophobia

Sanguivoriphobia

MEANING: fear of vampires

ORIGIN: the Latin word *sanguis*, meaning "blood"

Literally meaning "fear of blood eaters," SANGUIVORIPHOBIA is the extreme fear of vampires. This phobia occurs with the belief that vampires are real, subsisting on human blood and impervious to everything but a stake through the heart. Vampires appear in the folklore of many cultures; in 18th-century Eastern Europe, people were accused of vampirism. The many horror films and books that portray vampires, like Bram Stoker's *Dracula*, have done little to allay fears. Sanguivoriphobes experience dread, terror, and panic at the thought of vampires. Many sufferers keep their condition a secret, they avoid vampire movies, and, in some cases, refuse to go outside at night. Acute sufferers may become convinced that there are vampires roaming the planet and are highly suspicious of people with heliophobia (fear of the sun, also known as the vampire phobia).

THINGS TO AVOID: *Dracula* (book and films); the Twilight franchise; vampire bats; Transylvania; Anne Rice novels; *Buffy the Vampire Slayer*.

|||| Phobia Trivia ||||

Sanguivoriphobia is a branch of teratophobia, which is the fear of monsters in general. Bram Stoker's famous 1897 book

Dracula is thought to be based in part on Vlad III Dracula, also known as Vlad the Impaler. Between 1456 and 1462 he ruled Wallachia (present-day Romania and neighbor to Transylvania). During his six-year reign, Vlad is estimated to have killed up to 100,000 people, frequently using his favorite method of impaling victims on sharp wooden stakes. He was eventually arrested and imprisoned by the king of Hungary.

||||| Statistics |||||

The vampire bat is the only mammal that survives solely on blood, drinking the equivalent of about half its body weight each day. They are so light and agile that they are often able to drink blood from a sleeping animal for over 30 minutes without waking it up, enough to make even the toughest sanguivori-phobe squirm.

Scopophobia

MEANING: fear of being stared at

ORIGIN: the Greek word *skopein*, meaning "to look or examine"

Also known as scoptophobia or ophthalmophobia, SCOPOPHOBIA is the morbid fear of being watched or stared at by others. Often caused by an incidence of public ridicule, it is also prevalent in people with a physical deformity that they worry is likely to be stared at. Stage fright or a fear of public speaking also contribute to the phobia, as can low self-esteem or poor body image. Many scopophobes have the feeling that they are being watched all the time and avoid being out in public, often leaving them with little or no social life. Meeting new people is difficult, as is answering a phone in public. Blushing is a common symptom, which can cause the onset of erythrophobia (the fear of blushing), compounding the anxiety. Left untreated, scopophobia can escalate from a fear of being stared at by strangers to terror even at the gaze of close friends and family. Desensitization involves being stared at by strangers for increasingly prolonged periods, either resolving the issue or, in some cases, driving the person stark-raving mad.

THINGS TO AVOID: public spaces; public transit; dressing in bright clothes; Francis Ford Coppola's 1974 film *The Conversation*, in which the main character exhibits symptoms of scopophobia; Alfred Hitchcock's 1954 film *Rear Window*; the song "Scopophobia" by metal band *War from a Harlots Mouth*; the film *Sliver*.

||||| Phobia Trivia |||||

Sigmund Freud referred to scopophobia as a "dread of the evil eye."

||||| Statistics |||||

According to the Social Phobia/Social Anxiety Association, 7 percent of the American population has a social phobia like scopophobia.

Scriptophobia

MEANING: fear of writing in public

ORIGIN: the Latin word *script*, meaning "write"

While many writers take pride in their work, those with SCRIPTOPHOBIA are afraid of writing in public and other people reading it. Writing can be a very personal effort that exposes the writer's vulnerability. For scriptophobes, this vulnerability causes extreme anxiety; just the idea of having their words read by someone else is a devastating prospect. The phobia may come from the fear of rejection, criticism, or ridicule. Lack of self-esteem can also trigger the fear. Scriptophobes are guarded about what they write and tend to have poor handwriting that is difficult for others to read. The idea of writing in view of others can cause nausea, weeping, and fainting, leading scriptophobic students to skip school or even drop out. Adult sufferers are unable to take up occupations that require writing. For sufferers, writing in public feels akin to being naked in public (and those with gymnophobia, the fear of nudity, face a real problem if they ever find themselves needing to write while naked in public). So the next time you're denied an autograph by your favorite celebrity, it might just be that he or she is suffering a bout of scriptophobia.

THINGS TO AVOID: school; any occupation that requires writing in front of other people (don't forget that servers have to write down food orders, cops scribble traffic tickets all day long, and math teachers have to write equations on the board); board games, becoming a graffiti artist.

|||| Phobia Trivia ||||

Graphophobia, the more specific fear of handwriting, is similar to scriptophobia. It's from the Greek word *grapho*, meaning "write" or "draw."

An estimated $12 billion a year is spent cleaning up graffiti in America.

Selenophobia

MEANING: fear of the moon

ORIGIN: the Greek word *seleno*, meaning "moon"

Also known as lunaphobia (*luna* is Latin for "moon"), SELENOPHOBIA is the fear of the moon, sometimes including moonlight. The full moon is the source of particular terror for selenophobes. The lunar effect, as it's known, is the moon's influence on human behavior and, whether real or imaginary (though studies show that accidents and crime rates increase during a full moon), is a source of fear for those with selenophobia. Sufferers experience chills, dizziness, and the inability to articulate words, all of which become more acute as dusk approaches. Some selenophobes refuse to venture outside at night and close all the curtains to block out moonlight. Treatment includes gradual exposure to the moon, first a sliver before working up to a full moon. Learning that the moon is around 238,855 miles from Earth and more than likely has no supernatural features can also help. One moon-related fact that IS scary: Some experts believe that the moon influences a woman's menstrual cycle, including premenstrual mood swings. Selenophobia aside, that is pretty scary.

THINGS TO AVOID: cloudless nights; the songs "Blue Moon," "Man on the Moon," "Bad Moon Rising" (which features particularly ominous lyrics), and "Moonshadow" (another song with an especially threatening moon); the expression "once in a blue moon"; werewolf movies like *Teen Wolf* and *An American Werewolf in London*.

|||| Phobia Trivia ||||

Whether or not the moon is visible during the day depends on the phase of the lunar cycle. When approaching the new moon phase, the moon is too close to the sun for us to see it, as the light from the sun overpowers it. When nearing the full moon phase, it is opposite the sun and it becomes visible only at night. The best time to see the moon during the day is during its first and last quarters, when the moon is 90 degrees away from the sun.

|||| Statistics ||||

The moon is roughly a quarter of Earth's size and takes 27.3 days to complete its orbit. It is believed the moon was formed 4.5 billion years ago, when a rock crashed into Earth, creating debris that clumped together to make the moon.

Siderodromophobia

MEANING: fear of trains

ORIGIN: the Greek words *sideros*, meaning "iron," and *dromos*, meaning "racecourse"

SIDERODROMOPHOBIA is the fear of trains, railways, or railway travel. It's easy to see how trains can be a source of fear: They're large, noisy, and usually crowded, with screeching brakes and sudden jerking and swaying motions. Combined with their speed, their seemingly out-of-control motion can instill fear of derailment or catastrophe. High-profile train crashes and terrorist attacks also contribute to siderodromophobia, as can the thought of being stuck on the track as a train approaches. Sufferers avoid trains, refuse to cross railway tracks, and won't enter train stations; some even stay away from theme parks and museums with train rides or model trains. Even the sound of a train whistle is sometimes enough to induce sweating, crying, or freezing on the spot (not ideal if you happen to be standing on a railway track).

THINGS TO AVOID: trains and train stations; conductors; *Thomas and Friends*; the 1913 short story "Terror," about a man who suffers from the morbid fear of train travel; reading theories by Sigmund Freud (see Phobia Trivia below); the numerous country songs about trains.

|||| Phobia Trivia ||||

Siderodromophobia is a subclass of ochophobia, the fear of vehicles. Sigmund Freud believed siderodromophobia occurred because of an association of railway travel with sexuality due to the pleasurable sensation of shaking during train travel. He postulated that a sexually repressed person experiences anxiety when confronted with trains or railway travel. Freud himself suffered siderodromophobia. Take from that what you will.

America has the largest and most extensive network of railways in the world, totaling nearly 142,000 miles (80 percent of which is for freight transport). The longest train ride you can take without changing trains is 6,346 miles, from Moscow to Pyongyang. The journey takes nearly eight days.

Sidonglobophobia

MEANING: fear of cotton balls

ORIGIN: the Latin word *globi*, meaning "globe" or "sphere"

SIDONGLOBOPHOBIA is the extreme fear of cotton balls. Thought to affect only a handful of people around the world, this sensory phobia may arise from the resemblance of cotton balls to the eggs of creepy creatures like snakes, cockroaches, and lizards. Most sufferers, however, are creeped out by cotton balls' fluffy texture or the sound they make when rubbed together or torn apart. Some sidonglobophobes have trouble opening packages for fear of encountering these soft, light objects; others recoil at the thought of using a cotton swab or opening a new bottle of painkillers. Contact with cotton, no matter how soft, can lead to crying, hysterical screaming, and thoughts of death. Luckily, there are a number of treatment options available for this debilitating condition, including hypnotism, psychotherapy, gradual exposure therapy (although this should only be carried out under expert supervision), and medication. If left untreated, sidonglobophobes can descend into panic over the sheer number of cotton balls that are out there, just waiting to attack. Obviously, this condition is far more serious for women sufferers, as cotton balls are key instruments in removing both makeup and nail polish.

THINGS TO AVOID: removing nail polish; drug stores; pill bottles; clouds that look like cotton balls; marshmallows.

||||| Phobia Trivia |||||

For unknown reasons, many South Pacific islanders have an acute fear of cotton balls. Sidonglobophobia is also known as bambakophobia, from the Greek word *bambaki*, meaning "cotton." Michael Jackson is believed to have suffered from this fear.

||||| Statistics |||||

The fiber from a 500-pound cotton bale can produce 680,000 cotton balls—a little something for any sidonglobophobe cotton baler to ponder.

Sinistrophobia

MEANING: fear of the left or left-handed

ORIGIN: the Latin word *sinistro*, meaning "left"

SINISTROPHOBIA is the morbid fear of the left or of left-handed people. Sinistrophobes go to extreme measures to avoid anything to do with the left, lest they experience anxiety, rapid breathing, dizziness, and outright panic. This fear goes back to early Roman superstition about the left representing evil. The word "sinister," in fact, derives from the Latin word meaning "left." Left-handed people have been accused of witchcraft, and Satanists embrace the "left-handed path," that is, the dark and sinister sides of magic and mysticism. This long history of negative associations with the left might cause sinistrophobia. It may also arise as the result of a traumatic experience, like getting punched by a southpaw or having your pitch get homered out of the ballpark by a leftie. The issue might just come down to envy: Studies have found that there are more left-handed people with an IQ over 140 than right-handed people. Famous lefties include Albert Einstein, Charles Darwin, Benjamin Franklin, and Isaac Newton.

THINGS TO AVOID: Rafael Nadal; Rocky Balboa (except for a brief orthodox stint in *Rocky II*); power saws (more than 2,500 left-handed people are killed every year using equipment designed for right-handed people); August 13, which is Left-Handers Day.

|||| Phobia Trivia ||||

Sinistrophobia is related to (and sometimes used interchangeably with) levophobia (the fear of objects at the left side of the body). Dextrophobia is the fear of objects at the right side of the body (and shares origins with the word "dexterity"). The expression "start off on the wrong foot" comes from the Romans. A 1st-century decree ordered that no person enter or leave a building by their left foot. Guards were posted to ensure the order was adhered to, but most people were so scared of the left that it wasn't a problem.

|||| Statistics ||||

Around 10 percent of the world's population is left-handed. Eight U.S. presidents have been left-handed, most recently Barack Obama.

Somniphobia

MEANING: fear of sleep

ORIGIN: the Latin word *somni*, meaning "sleep"

SOMNIPHOBIA is the fear of going to sleep. It is often related to fear of the unknown, loss of control, or recurring nightmares. People who sleepwalk or talk in their sleep can develop somniphobia, fearful about what they'll do when they're unconscious. The association of death with sleep is a source of fear for some, as are horror films like *A Nightmare on Elm Street*. The thought of sleeping can produce nervousness, trembling, and, ironically, sleepiness in some somniphobes; many sufferers choose to work at night because they find it easier to sleep during the day. Sleep deprivation can lead to inability to concentrate, frequent illness, memory loss, irritability, and low energy levels that affect the sufferer's personal and professional life. In addition to cognitive therapy, relaxation techniques such as meditation and yoga are often used. If those don't work, you could always try counting sheep, as long as you don't suffer from zoophobia (the fear of animals).

THINGS TO AVOID: beds; excessive alcohol consumption; late-night movies; warm rooms; warm milk.

|||| Phobia Trivia ||||

Somniphobia is also known as clinophobia or hypnophobia, from Hypnos, the Greek god of sleep. French singer Edith Piaf suffered from somniphobia, saying, "I fear sleep, as it is a form of death." Counting sheep as a sleep aid is based on the idea that envisioning an endless series of identical white sheep will induce boredom and sleep. It is thought to come from ancient shepherds who used communal grazing land. They were required to keep a close count of their flocks, and so religiously counted them every night before they went to sleep. The concept has appeared in literature as far back as the early 12th century.

According to a 2018 Gallup poll, Americans average 6.8 hours of sleep each night, down more than an hour from 1942, and less than the recommended seven to nine hours.

Stenophobia

MEANING: fear of narrow places

ORIGIN: the Greek word *steno*, meaning "narrow"

STENOPHOBIA is the fear of narrow places or things. This phobia usually stems from a scary experience, like hiking down a narrow canyon or having to cross a narrow bridge. It may also result from a sense of being smothered or trapped when in the confines of a narrow hallway, path, or room, especially if the sufferer also has claustrophobia (fear of enclosed spaces). Stenophobia affects people of all ages and sizes, but disproportionately afflicts bigger people with a higher chance of getting stuck in a narrow space. Stenophobes stick to wide, open spaces and exhibit anxiety, breathlessness, and vomiting should they find themselves in a narrow place. In extreme cases, sufferers avoid all narrow things, including narrow drinking glasses, being narrow-minded, and keeping on the straight and narrow.

THINGS TO AVOID: tunnels; the straight and narrow; narrow-minded people; Wild West standoffs, which are rife with narrowed eyes.

||||| Phobia Trivia |||||

While related to claustrophobia, stenophobia is quite uncommon. Actor Matthew McConaughey is a sufferer, specifically afraid of tunnels and revolving doors.

||||| Statistics |||||

Guinness World Records awarded the title of the world's narrowest street to an alley called Spreuerhofstraße in Reutlingen, Germany. The "street" runs between two houses and is only around a foot wide at its narrowest point.

Symbolophobia

MEANING: fear of symbolism

ORIGIN: the Latin word *symbolum*, meaning "creed" or "mark"

SYMBOLOPHOBIA is the fear of symbols or symbolism. Symbols, in this sense, include objects of worship, computer icons, and business logos. This ubiquity of symbols in our culture is a source of terror for symbolophobes. The disorder can be limited to the fear of a particular religious symbol, government logo, or gang insignia, or it can extend to the general fear of all symbols. In many cases, it is difficult to distinguish fear of the symbol from the fear of what it represents, making diagnosis tricky. Encounters with dreaded corporate logos, computer icons, or religious symbols can cause tremors, chest pain, and general panic. As for the analysis of symbolism in poetry or literature, well, it's not just symbolophobes who find that scary.

THINGS TO AVOID: computers and smartphones; the logos of nearly all companies; English class; religions and cults.

||||| Phobia Trivia |||||

One of history's most famous symbols is the swastika, formed by a cross with each of its arms bent at right angles. Reviled for its association with Nazis, the swastika has actually been around for thousands of years. The word *swastika* comes from the Sanskrit for any lucky or auspicious object. The symbol has been found on pottery dating as far back as 5000 BC; is a sacred religious symbol in Hinduism, Buddhism, and Jainism; and has been adopted across cultures that include Native Americans, Hittites, Celts, and ancient Greeks.

||||| Statistics |||||

The double-headed eagle motif is arguably the oldest symbol known to man, first appearing in the Early Bronze Age in Mesopotamia. It has been used throughout history by various cultures and continues to appear today on flags and coats of arms.

Symmetrophobia

MEANING: fear of symmetry

ORIGIN: the Greek words *sym*, meaning "same," and *metri*, meaning "measure"

SYMMETROPHOBIA is the unwarranted fear of symmetry or symmetrical things. While symmetry is widely acknowledged as a fundamental element of beauty in nature, architecture, and art, symmetrophobes dread it. Symmetrophobes tend to be chaotic in nature, and the condition can result from a subconscious aversion to authority or desire for visual disorder. Fear of perfection or insecurity over one's own imperfections can also play a role—sufferers may believe themselves not worthy of symmetry or beauty. Symmetrophobes avoid all things symmetrical, preferring things random and skewed. An abundance of symmetry causes shortness of breath, nausea, vomiting, and general disquietude. The condition is usually treated using cognitive psychotherapy or hypnosis. Because of their condition, symmetrophobes tend to be attracted to people who would not be considered attractive according to societal standards of beauty. But, as the saying goes, beauty is in the eye of the beholder, or the symmetrophobe in this case.

THINGS TO AVOID: nature; architecture; paintings and drawings, in particular Leonardo da Vinci's *The Vitruvian Man*; good-looking people.

||||| Phobia Trivia |||||

Symmetrophobia is the opposite of asymmetrophobia, the fear of asymmetrical things. The golden ratio (1:1.618) is a mathematical ratio that is commonly used in geometry, art, design, and nature that promotes a sense of beauty through harmony and proportion. It can be found in the Pyramids of Giza, the Parthenon, Michelangelo's Sistine Chapel ceiling, Da Vinci's *Mona Lisa*, and many company logos, from McDonald's to Pepsi. Our bodies and faces even follow the golden ratio; the more closely you exhibit it in your proportions, the better looking you are thought to be.

Statistics

In 2016, the faces of a number of female celebrities were analyzed using computer mapping technology to determine their symmetry. Amber Heard topped the list, with facial symmetry of 91.85 percent. Kim Kardashian was second, with 91.39 percent, and Kate Moss third, with 91.06 percent. Marilyn Monroe came in ninth, at 89.41 percent.

Is for
Triskaidekaphobia

Taphophobia

MEANING: fear of being buried alive

ORIGIN: the Greek word *taphos*, meaning "grave" or "tomb"

Sometimes spelled "taphephobia," TAPHOPHOBIA is the irrational fear of being buried alive, specifically as a result of being incorrectly pronounced dead. Sufferers avoid cemeteries, horror movies, wakes, coffins, and enclosed spaces like basements, caves, and underground areas. Extreme taphophobes make elaborate arrangements for their own funerals, outfitting their coffins with air pipes, oxygen tanks, and heart stimulators. Others request burial at least three days after death. There is some basis for this fear. The 19th century saw numerous cases of people accidentally buried alive. Sometimes people were in a coma or had passed out, only to wake up and find themselves underground. To this end, a rope was tied to the toe of some corpses in their coffins, which was attached to a bell above ground. If the "deceased" woke up, the bell could be rung and the person saved. The expressions "saved by the bell" and "dead ringer" derive from this practice. The phobia can also arise from a genuine fear of graves or in relation to claustrophobia (the fear of enclosed spaces). Relaxation techniques, such as yoga, tai chi, and meditation are generally used to treat the condition, as is the gradual exposure to cemeteries and graves.

THINGS TO AVOID: cemeteries; coffins; open graves; funerals; *Kill Bill: Volume 2*; a number of Edgar Allen Poe's works.

A number of celebrities have suffered from taphophobia. Edgar Allen Poe wrote about it in several of his works, and on his deathbed George Washington made his attendants promise not to bury him for two days. Referring to a scene in *Kill Bill: Volume 2,* where she is buried alive in a coffin, Uma Thurman told *Daily Mail* reporters, "There was no acting required. Real screams available. It was horrific. Nobody wants to live that experience." Taphophobia is closely related to thanatophobia (the fear of death), placophobia (the fear of tombstones), claustrophobia (the fear of enclosed spaces), and coimetrophobia (the fear of cemeteries), a condition Sarah Michelle Gellar suffers from, despite her role in *Buffy the Vampire Slayer.*

The earliest evidence of a wooden coffin was found in Shaanxi Province, China. The coffin was dated to 5000 BC.

Tapinophobia

MEANING: fear of being contagious

ORIGIN: unknown

TAPINOPHOBIA is the fear of being contagious. While it's common to fear getting sick, tapinophobes fear passing illness on to others, usually out of fear that they will be blamed or ridiculed. Perfectionists are particularly susceptible; they see having an ailment and passing it on as a fault or imperfection. Tapinophobes go to great lengths to avoid getting sick, getting vaccinated, taking vitamin supplements, constantly washing their hands, and sometimes even wearing a mask. Most sufferers experience extreme anxiety even with the mildest of colds, isolating themselves the moment they suspect they're coming down with something that might be contagious. Untreated, tapinophobia affects quality of life and can cause breathlessness, nausea, depression, and, most concerning of all, sleepiness. After all, yawning is very contagious.

THINGS TO AVOID: leaving the house; winter in large cities; the American frontier during colonization.

||||| Phobia Trivia |||||

Around 95 percent of the 50 million native people living in the Americas were killed by diseases brought by European colonists, and yet few Europeans were killed by Native American diseases. This is because a significant percentage of human diseases come from domestic animals. Europeans had been surrounded by domestic animals for thousands of years and had grown immune. Living in large, densely developed populations also contributed to a robust European immune system. In the end, the West was not won by firepower, but by contagious diseases.

||||| Statistics |||||

The World Health Organization reports that the most deadly contagious disease is lower-respiratory infection, which caused 3 million deaths worldwide in 2016.

Taurophobia

MEANING: fear of bulls

ORIGIN: the Latin word *tauro*, meaning "bull"

TAUROPHOBIA is the extreme fear of bulls. A symbol of power and aggression, these heavily muscled animals' deadly horns and flared nostrils can elicit terror, as can the stamping of their hooves. Bulls are used in a number of particularly brutal traditions and forms of entertainment, including bullfighting, Pamplona's running of the bulls, and rodeos. Witnessing a bull-related tragedy (a matador or bull rider getting killed, for example) at one of these spectacles can bring about taurophobia. The sight of a bull induces trembling and panic attacks, and sufferers avoid cattle ranches and other places where bulls may roam. Gradual desensitization is the most common form of treatment, but coming face to face with a bull is not recommended in the early stages of treatment. The idea that bulls are compelled to charge at the color red is a myth; they're actually attracted to the movement of the matador's cape, not its color. So if you do find yourself facing off with a snorting titan bent on destruction, forget what you're wearing and just try to control the urge to move.

THINGS TO AVOID: bullrings; Spain; France; cattle ranches.

Similar to taurophobia is bovinophobia (from *bovi*, the Latin word for "ox" or "cattle"), which is the fear of cows or cattle.

Since 1700, approximately 325 matadors have been killed in the arena. And in the running of the bulls in Pamplona, Spain, 15 people have been killed since its inception in 1924.

Thalassophobia

MEANING: fear of the ocean

ORIGIN: the Greek word *thalassa*, meaning "sea"

THALASSOPHOBIA is the irrational fear of the sea. It includes the fear of other large bodies of water, ocean waves, or being a great distance from land, and might arise after witnessing a drowning or other tragedy at sea. Other sources of fear include dangerous sea creatures (like sharks, electric eels, and giant squid), the sinking of mighty ships (most notably the *Titanic*), and the mysteries of its vast, largely unexplored depths. Books and films that depict the dangers of the sea, including *20,000 Leagues Under the Sea*, *Moby-Dick*, and *Jaws*, do very little to allay terror. Some thalassophobes appreciate the beauty and majesty of the sea, but panic if anywhere near the shoreline, while others can't even bear to see pictures of it. Thalassophobes should understand that, occasional gruesome shark attack aside, oceans are generally safe and enjoyable places to be. Instances of death at sea are far less common than (hodophobes, look away) road accidents.

THINGS TO AVOID: the seven oceans; the innumerable seas; other large bodies of water; *Jaws* (book and film); *Moby-Dick* (book and film); *20,000 Leagues Under the Sea*; the movie *Titanic*; Caribbean vacations.

||||| Phobia Trivia |||||

"Aquaphobia" and "hydrophobia" are sometimes used in place or thalassophobia. Aquaphobia, however, is the fear of all kinds of water (including bathtub water), while hydrophobia, which develops in the advanced stages of rabies, is a fear of drinking water. Michael Jordan has been a thalassophobe since witnessing the death of a childhood friend by drowning. Carmen Electra, who played a lifeguard in the hit show *Baywatch*, can't swim and is afraid of the sea.

||||| Statistics |||||

The oceans cover over 70 percent of Earth's surface and contain 94 percent of its living species. To date, less than 5 percent of our oceans have been explored.

Tonsurephobia

MEANING: fear of getting a haircut

ORIGIN: the Greek word *tonsure*, meaning "to cut"

TONSUREPHOBIA is the overwhelming fear of getting a haircut. Predominantly suffered by children, the condition usually begins with a bad haircut experience, being forced to sit still for a long period, or schoolyard bullying because of a bad haircut. Tonsurephobia may also be rooted in fear of sharp blades snipping away close to the face and ears, or that hair won't grow back after being cut too short. Most sufferers avoid haircuts at all costs; children with the condition might refuse to sit still and have to be physically restrained at haircut time. Long, unkempt hair can lead to problems in a professional setting and, of course, split ends. Exposure therapy involves desensitizing sufferers to the tools of grooming, including buzzing electric clippers, pointy scissors, and incredibly sharp razors. Failing that, there's always the option of going for the world record for longest hair.

THINGS TO AVOID: barbers; hairdressers; the military; clippers; scissors; razors; the film *Edward Scissorhands*.

|||| Phobia Trivia ||||

Timothy Leary, the American psychologist and psychedelic drug advocate, suffered tonsurephobia, cutting his own hair because of his fear of barbers. Oslo, Norway, is the most expensive place for a haircut, averaging nearly $100 for both men and women.

|||| Statistics ||||

According to *Guinness World Records*, the most consecutive haircuts completed in 24 hours by an individual is 526, achieved by Nabi Salehi in London in 2011.

Triskaidekaphobia

MEANING: fear of the number 13

ORIGIN: the Greek word *triskaideka*, meaning "thirteen"

Coined by American psychiatrist Isador Coriat in his 1910 book *Abnormal Psychology*, TRISKAIDEKAPHOBIA is the fear of the number 13. Some attribute the number's association with evil to the idea that Judas Iscariot, the man who betrayed Jesus, was the 13th apostle. Today, many airlines, restaurants, and hotels avoid the number 13; flight numbers don't contain the number 13, and some hotels skip from the 12th to the 14th floor. Something bad happening on the 13th day of a month might cause triskaidekaphobia. The superstition has a significant impact on the economy: Many people refuse to do business or even go to work on the 13th. Sufferers go to extreme lengths to avoid the number 13, refusing to fly, drive, or leave home on the 13th for fear that bad luck might be lurking.

THINGS TO AVOID: channel 13; the 13th floor; flights with 13 in the number; leaving home or doing anything else on the 13th of the month.

||||| Phobia Trivia |||||

Franklin D. Roosevelt was a triskaidekaphobe, as is horror novelist Stephen King. Fear of Friday the 13th is an even more specific phobia known as paraskevidekatriaphobia (*paraskevi* is the Greek word for "Friday"). But it's not all bad news for the much-maligned numeral. Thirteen is considered lucky in Italy, and it's a lucky number in Cantonese-speaking areas like Macau and Hong Kong, where it sounds similar to the word meaning "sure to live," as opposed to unlucky number 14, which sounds like "sure to die."

While around 10 percent of Americans are superstitious about the number 13, not all are considered triskaidekaphobes. An extreme aversion is required to qualify for this uniquely angst-ridden group.

Trypophobia

MEANING: fear of holes

ORIGIN: the Greek word *trypa*, meaning "hole"

Thought to be more prevalent in women than in men, TRYPOPHOBIA is the fear of holes, particularly the sight of irregular patterns or asymmetrical clusters of small holes or bumps. A largely unexplored phobia, researchers believe that trypophobia may be triggered by a biological revulsion that associates pockmarked shapes or patterns with danger and disease. There is some evidence to support this theory, as holes in organic matter are often an indication of disease; rashes or blisters on the skin might indicate infections or diseases such as measles, and small holes in produce can be caused by insects or parasites. Unfortunately for the trypophobe, innocuous things like sponges, wood, and honeycomb can produce panic and the feeling of skin "crawling." Facing the fear of tiny holes is the best way to overcome it.

THINGS TO AVOID: honeycomb; sponges; rash-ridden folk; acne; some vegetables and fruits; the episode of *American*

Horror Story that featured a trypophobic character (in fact, trypophobia-inducing advertising was used to promote the episode, which allegedly disturbed a number of trypophobes).

The term is believed to have been coined online in 2005. Since then, the concept of trypophobia has become popular on social media, where self-diagnosed trypophobes assemble to share and discuss their experiences.

Trypophobia is not yet considered an official phobia; more people experience disgust, rather than extreme fear, at the sight of small holes.

Turophobia

MEANING: fear of cheese

ORIGIN: the Greek word *turi*, meaning "cheese"

TUROPHOBIA is an irratio-
nal fear of cheese that goes
far beyond a simple distaste for it. A turophobe might fear a particular type of cheese, or might be frightened of all cheeses, from Asiago to Yorkshire blue. The fear of cheese can stem from its gooey texture or pungent smell, or might be caused by a traumatic cheese-related incident, like a food fight gone wrong. Crumbly cheeses are deeply off-putting to some sufferers; others are upset by the thought of the mess that gooey cheese can make, which may be related to

obsessive-compulsive disorder. Turophobes avoid supermarkets and restaurants, where the sight or smell of cheese can cause vomiting or a cold sweat. More extreme sufferers are nauseated by the words "cheese" and "cheesy." Most turophobes report that the scariest cheeses are soft ones, like camembert, and strong-smelling blue varieties, such as stilton. But by far the worst part of turophobia is pretty obvious: Imagine having to eat cheeseless pizza.

THINGS TO AVOID: restaurants and fast food establishments; supermarkets, grocery stores, and delis; cooking shows; France; Italy; being photographed in the English-speaking world ("Say cheese!").

||||| Phobia Trivia |||||

Cheesemaking is thought to go back to 8000 BC, when sheep were first domesticated. It was certainly a sophisticated enterprise by the time of the Roman Empire. As for the expression "say cheese," the origins are uncertain, but historians believe that Franklin D. Roosevelt may have been the first to coin it. Whatever the origins, it's an improvement on the less jovial 19th-century expression that was used to obtain a more austere expression—"say prunes."

||||| Statistics |||||

According to 2017 data from the U.S. Department of Agriculture, the average American consumed about 15 pounds of American cheese and nearly 22 pounds of imported cheese that year.

Tyrannophobia

MEANING: fear of tyrants

ORIGIN: the Greek word *tyrann*, meaning "dictator"

TYRANNOPHOBIA is the fear of tyrants or dictators, and manifests as the fear of certain political leaders, as well as fear of someone who exhibits the qualities of a tyrant, like a teacher, employer, or parent. This phobia affects people with low self-esteem and is often caused by a traumatic experience of being severely reprimanded or punished. Tyrannophobes tend to be submissive, accepting ridicule and abuse without protest. They are shy and fear social situations, sometimes avoiding people altogether and becoming reclusive. Contact with anyone dictatorial or overbearing causes tremors, breathlessness, and nausea. In extreme cases, the condition is treated with medication. Tyrannophobes planning to visit North Korea any time soon had better take a double dose.

THINGS TO AVOID: dictators like Adolf Hitler (Germany), Joseph Stalin (Soviet Union), Mao Zedong (China), Benito Mussolini (Italy), Pol Pot (Cambodia), Saddam Hussein (Iraq), Robert Mugabe (Zimbabwe), Kim Jong-un (North Korea), Fidel Castro (Cuba), and Idi Amin (Uganda); documentaries about dictators; dictatorial friends, teachers, and parents.

|||| Phobia Trivia ||||

Though they sound similar, tyrannophobia has nothing to do with tyrannosaurusphobia, the fear of the *Tyrannosaurus rex* dinosaur, a branch of zoophobia (the fear of animals). Given that humans didn't coexist with dinosaurs, it is hard to know how that phobia develops. Should you somehow encounter a

T. rex, however, you'd probably come down with tyrannosaurusphobia pretty quickly.

|||| Statistics ||||

Fidel Castro's run as head of state lasted from January 8, 1959, to April 19, 2011.

Is for Urophobia

Uranophobia

MEANING: fear of heaven

ORIGIN: the Greek word *uranos*, meaning "heaven"

Also spelled "ouranophobia," URANOPHOBIA is the fear of heaven. Many religious people hope to go to heaven after they die. Uranophobes, on the other hand, are terrified at the idea of meeting their creator, being judged and punished for their sins. Others are scared of angels, with their human bodies and disconcertingly gigantic wings. Still other sufferers fear the unknown mysteries that heaven might hold. Uranophobes avoid talking about death and the afterlife, and refuse to go to church or read the Bible lest thoughts of heaven enter their minds. Uranophobia must be a potent fear, especially given that the alternative to heaven involves fire, burning, heat, and a lot of other nasty stuff.

THINGS TO AVOID: songs with "heaven" in the title; the Bible; churches; television evangelists.

Uranophobia is related to a number of other phobias, including anablephobia (the fear of looking up), apeirophobia (the fear of infinity), angelophobia (the fear of angels), zeusophobia (the fear of god), and stygiophobia (the fear of hell).

Studies vary, but approximately 70 percent of Americans (and presumably 100 percent of uranophobes) believe in heaven.

Urophobia

MEANING: fear of urination

ORIGIN: the Greek word *ouro*, meaning "urine"

Sometimes referred to as paruresis or shy bladder syndrome, UROPHOBIA is the fear of urine or urination. Thought to affect more men than women, the main causes of this condition are the unpleasant odor of urine after excretion, as well as experiencing pain while urinating. Another cause can be a past trauma related to urine, such as an uncouth school bathroom prank. Since urine is yellow in color (particularly after the consumption of vitamin supplements), sufferers of xanthophobia (the fear of yellow) can also develop urophobia. Anxiety and emotional turmoil around urination are highly disruptive to daily function. Inability to pee in a public toilet makes it impossible to attend big spectacles or sporting events, especially when the consumption of alcohol is involved. People with the condition may limit their fluid intake to avoid urination, which can lead to physical problems like kidney stones, urinary tract infections, and bed-wetting. Hypnotherapy is commonly used to treat this condition.

THINGS TO AVOID: public toilets; drinking in public.

Related to urophobia is katourophobia, which is the fear of the word "piss."

The average person will urinate over 230,000 times by age 80, expelling nearly half a million liters of urine.

Is for Vestiphobia

Veloxrotaphobia

MEANING: fear of roller coasters

ORIGIN: the Latin word *velox*, meaning "swift" or "rapid"

Some people feel dizzy, nauseated, unsafe, and terrified by roller coasters, and they're not even the ones riding. More commonly known as coasterphobia, VELOXROTAPHOBIA is the extreme fear of roller coasters. Veloxrotaphobia is sometimes linked to acrophobia (the fear of heights), claustrophobia (the fear of enclosed spaces), or emetophobia (the fear of vomiting). Witnessing or being involved with a mechanical failure or tragedy on a roller coaster is also likely to cause the phobia. The very names of the rides (Gravitron, Death Ride, Mind Eraser) evoke fear, as can standing in line to buy tickets. Symptoms include rapid breathing, sweating, nausea, and sheer panic; most veloxrotaphobes avoid theme parks at any cost. Exposure therapy presumably starts with the tiny rides meant for toddlers before working up to anything involving a carriage full of screaming people hurtling around multiple loops hundreds of feet from the ground. While the fear of roller coasters has some legitimate merit, veloxrotaphobia is not yet an officially recognized phobia.

THINGS TO AVOID: theme parks; my book *Why Do Roller Coasters Make You Puke?*; the film *Final Destination 3*.

|||| Phobia Trivia ||||

The world's first roller coaster opened on Brooklyn's Coney Island in 1884. Designed by LaMarcus Thompson, it traveled at 6 miles per hour and cost a nickel to ride.

Kingda Ka, in New Jersey's Six Flags Great Adventure park, is the tallest roller coaster in the world; the fastest is Formula Rossa at Ferrari World in Abu Dhabi. The Gravity Max ride in Taiwan's Lihpao Land park is widely regarded as the world's scariest roller coaster.

Vestiphobia

MEANING: fear of clothing

ORIGIN: the Latin word *vestis*, meaning "clothing," "garment," or "covering"

VESTIPHOBIA is the extreme fear of clothing. Clothing provides warmth, comfort, security, and, for the vestiphobe, severe panic attacks and social isolation. While some claim that vestiphobia is hereditary, it often stems from having had an allergic reaction to fabric or having been forced to wear uncomfortable or restrictive clothes. Being made to wear ugly clothes as a child (and facing ridicule for it) can spawn the phobia, as can the association of certain clothes with trauma (a soldier's uniform triggering PTSD, for example). The fear of clothing might be related to claustrophobia; sufferers can't stand garments that are tight, like ties or turtlenecks. Many vestiphobes wear oversized or loose clothing, or no clothing at all. Public nudity is socially unacceptable in most cultures, meaning that some vestiphobes are unable to leave their homes. But at least they'll save money on wardrobe (and find themselves with extra storage space).

THINGS TO AVOID: public places; cold environments; fashion shows; department stores; *Project Runway*.

Phobia Trivia

Despite their frequent nudity, most porn stars are not technically vestiphobes, nor are most nudists. The opposite of vestiphobia is gymnophobia, the fear of nudity.

Statistics

It is believed that humans first began wearing clothing, in the form of animal skins, 500,000 years ago, an unfortunate turning point for ancient vestiphobes.

Is for Wiccaphobia

Wiccaphobia

MEANING: fear of witches

ORIGIN: the Old English word *wicca*, meaning "witch"

WICCAPHOBIA is the intense fear of witches or witchcraft (and is not the fear of Wikipedia, unless you're reading the page about witches). This phobia began as far back as the 14th century, when women accused of witchcraft were punished by draconian means, including burning at the stake. Historically thought to be evil and associated with Satan and the dark arts, witches are served no better by the modern image of a black-clad woman with a crooked nose, warts, and cauldron full of newts' eyes (anyone else scared yet?). Fear of witches affects people from certain religious upbringings, as well as those for whom the notion of the scary witch was prevalent in child-hood stories, movies, and TV shows. Sufferers stay home on Halloween and avoid witch haunts like graveyards and spooky forests, lest they run into a witch and get turned into a toad. Self-help groups and talk therapy are the best treatments, in addition to learning that witches are not real.

THINGS TO AVOID: Halloween; the film *The Witches of Eastwick*; the television series *Charmed*; broomsticks; *The Wizard of Oz*; black cats; cauldrons; the Eagles song "Witchy Woman"; the Frank Sinatra song "Witchcraft."

||||| Phobia Trivia |||||

It is estimated that around 50,000 people were executed for witchcraft in Europe and America between the 14th and 17th centuries. Common methods of execution were hanging, drowning, and burning. Burning was often favored as it was generally considered a more painful way to die. Clearly there were some pretty serious wiccaphobes back then.

If some statistics are to be believed, there are nearly 700,000 people practicing witchcraft in the world today.

Is for Xanthophobia

Xanthophobia

MEANING: fear of the color yellow

ORIGIN: the Greek word *xanthos*, meaning "yellow"

XANTHOPHOBIA is the irrational fear of the color yellow. While the color may seem innocuous, yellow has had many negative connotations throughout history. The American phrase "yellow belly" has been spat at cowards since the 1800s. At the same time, "yellow journalism" was used for newspapers with little or no legitimate news that instead used attention-grabbing headlines to sell papers (the equivalent of today's clickbait). The color of treachery, yellow-painted doors identified traitors in medieval France, and the robes of Judas Iscariot, the man who betrayed Jesus, are frequently yellow in paintings. Traumatic events can trigger the condition, like being hit by a school bus or stung by a bee. Acute sufferers refuse to eat anything yellow and may even close their eyes when urinating, and avoid places with brightly colored lights, such as Las Vegas.

THINGS TO AVOID: sunny days; flowers; the Coldplay song "Yellow"; cheese; lemons; baby chickens (especially if you also suffer from alektorophobia, the fear of chickens); bananas; corn; canaries; egg yolks; buses and tractors; taxicabs; The Beatles' "Yellow Submarine"; yellow submarines; phone books.

||||| Phobia Trivia |||||

Across much of the Western world, yellow is associated with humor, amusement, and joy, but also with jealousy, greed, duplicity, and cowardice. In many Asian countries it is the color of harmony, wisdom, and happiness, while in Iran it is associated with wisdom, but also sickness. Yellow is clearly a very versatile color.

A 2011 survey conducted by Dulux Paints found that the most popular color is blue, followed by red and green. Yellow was the least favorite of the major colors, preferred by only 5 percent of people.

Xenoglossophobia

MEANING: fear of foreign languages

ORIGIN: the Latin words *xeno*, meaning "foreign," and *glosso*, meaning "tongue" or "language"

XENOGLOSSOPHOBIA is the irrational fear of foreign languages, which tends to develop while trying to learn a language. The difficulty in mastering a language, as well as the performance anxiety around being evaluated in a classroom setting, can cause the phobia. Learning a language can lead to an identity crisis, particularly when already living abroad in a country where you haven't mastered the language. Xenoglossophobia can also arise out of fear that one's language skills are inadequate for an emergency situation (finding oneself in Mexico, for example, and being unable to order a margarita when you desperately need one). Xenoglossophobes in a foreign country are at risk of becoming reclusive, isolated from locals, and unable to enter the workforce, while domestic sufferers avoid talking to foreigners and never travel abroad. Psychotherapy and relaxation techniques are often used to treat the issue.

Medication is required in extreme cases, because, if left untreated, xenoglossophobes will never get that margarita.

THINGS TO AVOID: foreign travel; tourists; foreign television and radio stations; subtitled movies; language classes.

The most spoken languages in the world are Mandarin then Spanish, with English third. Of the world's 7.5 billion inhabitants, about 360 million speak English as their first language, which is about 5 percent.

There are around 6,500 spoken languages, though approximately 2,000 of these have fewer than 1,000 speakers.

Xerophobia

MEANING: fear of dryness

ORIGIN: the Greek word *xero*, meaning "dry"

XEROPHOBIA is the fear of dryness or dry places, which can include deserts, dehydration, dry skin, cracked lips, or the sound of fingernails on a chalkboard. An outgrowth of our innate knowledge that hydration is essential to sustaining life, xerophobia is the extreme version of an evolutionarily based fear. Having experienced extreme dehydration can also result in xerophobia. Xerophobes avoid dry climates, use moisturizing creams excessively, and drink copious amounts of water. Severe sufferers even shun people with dry skin, hair, or lips. Treatment involves educating the patient that dryness is a temporary state that can be reversed. This has a high success rate, except in cases where the sufferer is also a cenosillica-phobe (has the fear of an empty beer glass) and they can't get a refill.

THINGS TO AVOID: deserts; Death Valley; Antarctica; Atacama Desert.

|||| Phobia Trivia ||||

While Death Valley averages just 2.36 inches of rain each year, the driest place in the world (outside of Antarctica) is Chile's Atacama Desert. Some parts have not had rain in over 500 years. The wettest place in the world is India's Mawsynram village, with an average 467 inches per year.

|||| Statistics ||||

Australia is the smallest of the world's continents and, apart from Antarctica, the driest.

Xocolatophobia

MEANING: fear of chocolate

ORIGIN: the Nahuatl words *xococ*, meaning "sour" or "bitter," and *atl*, meaning "water" or "drink"

XOCOLATOPHOBIA is the extreme fear of chocolate. While the fear of chocolate might seem unfathomable, sufferers find the stuff unbearable to smell or look at, let alone eat. Past overindulgence that led to sickness is a common cause. Other sufferers perceive chocolate as dirty, likening its color and texture to feces. Still others despise the bitter taste, fearing it might be poisonous (a legitimate fear if you're a horse, dog, or parrot; see Phobia Trivia below). Xocolatophobes avoid brownies, truffles, and cookies, and sometimes refuse to be in the presence of others who are eating chocolate, particularly tough at Christmas and Easter. Accidentally consuming chocolate results in heart palpitations, sweating, trembling, and panic. As many experts believe that chocolate has genuinely addictive qualities (see Phobia Trivia below), the xocolatophobe who inadvertently eats a delicious chocolate cake could then be faced with quite the dilemma.

THINGS TO AVOID: Easter, Christmas, and Halloween; birthdays; most desserts; supermarkets; cafés; *Chocolat* (book and film).

Phobia Trivia

Chocolate releases endorphins in the brain, which act like opiates to reduce sensitivity to pain. It also contains tryptophan, which enhances serotonin function and regulates moods, and phenylethylamine, which is said to produce an amphetamine-like high. However, chocolate also contains theobromine, which is toxic to horses, dogs, and parrots.

Statistics

In 2015, Americans ate nearly 18 percent of the world's chocolate, amounting to around $18.7 billion worth.

Xyrophobia

MEANING: fear of razors

ORIGIN: the Greek word *xyro*, meaning "razor"

XYROPHOBIA is the intense fear of razors. A common daily ritual, shaving occasionally results in cuts, bleeding, and pain. Xyrophobia results from a severe shaving injury or razor cut that got infected. It may also arise from the apprehension of shaving for the first time or losing a close friend or family member to razor-related trauma, like suicide or a razor-wielding murderer. Xyrophobes experience intense anxiety at the thought of using a razor and refuse to shave under any circumstances. Male sufferers resort to wearing a full beard, while women leave their legs and underarms unshaven. Some xyrophobes become ashamed and embarrassed by their unkempt appearance, leading to social withdrawal and isolation. Others embrace it, becoming hippies and moving to Central America to sit on street corners with a couple of dogs and play the guitar.

THINGS TO AVOID: straight razors, disposable razors, safety razors, and electric razors; barber shops.

|||| Phobia Trivia ||||

Razors have been used since prehistoric times: Cave paintings depict sharpened clamshells, shark teeth, and flint stones being used for shaving. The oldest razor-like object ever found is thought to date as far back as 18,000 BC. Excavations in Egypt unearthed copper and gold razors from 4000 BC.

|||| Statistics ||||

The Environmental Protection Agency estimates that 2 billion razors are thrown away each year in America. Perhaps there are more xyrophobes out there than we think.

Is for Ymophobia

Ymophobia

MEANING: fear of contrariety

ORIGIN: the Latin word *ymo*, meaning "contrary"

YMOPHOBIA is the fear of contrariety or being contrary. The argumentative tendencies of a contrarian can be irksome, but the ymophobe detests and actually fears them. Sufferers may have been traumatized by a heated argument with such a person. Others just despise contrariety so deeply that it turns into a fear. Encountering the devil's advocate causes sweatiness, breathlessness, extreme anxiety, and the desire to lash out verbally or even physically. Ymophobes avoid social gatherings, televised debates, the comments section, and the nursery rhyme "Mary, Mary, Quite Contrary."

THINGS TO AVOID: know-it-alls; devil's advocates; people who say "on the contrary" or use the French expression "au contraire"; politics; television debates; friendly debates; heated debates; other debating.

|||| Phobia Trivia ||||

Greek playwright Sophocles wrote in his 441 BC play *Antigone*: "All men make mistakes, but a good man yields when he knows his course is wrong, and repairs the evil. The only crime is pride."

|||| Statistics ||||

Contrariety is widely regarded as one of the most annoying personality traits.

Z

Is for Zemmiphobia

Zelophobia

MEANING: fear of jealousy

ORIGIN: the Greek word *zelo*, meaning "jealousy"

ZELOPHOBIA is the abnormal fear of jealousy and can extend to all intense emotions. Caused by childhood emotional or verbal abuse, the condition is more common in people who come from strict or repressive upbringings. It can also arise from adult relationship troubles, either having experienced intense jealously or having dealt with a highly jealous partner. Zelophobes repress loving emotions and avoid romantic relationships for fear of jealousy. Situations that provoke jealousy evoke nervousness and overwhelming feelings of being trapped. Zelophobes might exhibit anger and violence, ironically similar to the temperament of an extremely jealous person.

THINGS TO AVOID: flirty partners; the song "Jealous Lover"; dating models; Rick Springfield (if your name is Jesse).

Phobia Trivia

The color green's association with jealousy began in ancient Greece, where it was believed that various illnesses and "restless emotions" were accompanied by an overproduction of bile, which lent a pallid green color to a person's complexion; 7th-century poet Sappho described a stricken lover as "green." Shakespeare brought the idea to the mainstream when he coined the phrase "green-eyed monster."

Studies have found that there is no difference in levels of jealousy between men and women.

Zemmiphobia

MEANING: fear of the great mole rat

ORIGIN: the Slavic word *zemni*, meaning "of the Earth"

ZEMMIPHOBIA is an irrational fear of the great mole rat. The interesting thing about this irrational phobia is that there is no such animal as the great mole rat. Thus, it's an irrational phobia of a completely imaginary creature! The phobia more than likely relates to the naked mole rat (also known as the "sand puppy"), a burrowing rodent native to parts of East Africa. Despite the innocuous-sounding pseudonym given to this animal, it does actually have some pretty scary qualities. For starters, it is a hideous animal to look at. It has a plasticky, hairless pink body, with tightly shut beady eyes and two long protruding, fang-like teeth. This odious appearance is enough to instill fear in some people, but more than that are its other physical qualities. While only three to four inches long, it is highly adept at moving underground and can move backward as fast as it can forward. Its protruding teeth are powerful and large and are used for digging, and it can survive for up to five hours in air that contains virtually no oxygen, showing no apparent signs of distress. Living for up to 32 years, the record for any rodent, this bizarre mammal lives in colonies of up to 300 omnivorous rats. Incredibly, the naked mole rat is also resistant to cancer, and lacks pain sensitivity in its skin, making it an extremely formidable opponent if encountered at close quarters in its natural habitat. Given that this diminutive animal resides almost exclusively underground, a prior negative experience with a mole rat is fairly unlikely; a past incident with another type of aboveground hairless rodent could potentially result in the phobia. While exposure therapy is recommended to treat zemmiphobia, presumably thrusting the patient underground into a vast colony of these seemingly indestructible rodents is likely to have moderate to limited success.

THINGS TO AVOID: underground tunnels in parts of East Africa; *Kim Possible*; searching the internet for pictures of the great or naked mole rat as most of the images are rather disturbing, even to non-zemmiphobes; *The Princess Bride*, which features R.O.U.S.es, a species almost certainly akin to the imaginary great mole rat.

|||| Phobia Trivia ||||

Because of its remarkable characteristics, particularly in relation to cancer resistance, the journal *Science* named the naked mole rat the "Vertebrate of the Year" for 2013. Bravo.

|||| Statistics ||||

The mortality rate of the naked mole rat does not increase with age, they are widespread and numerous in parts of East Africa, and they are not considered threatened—more bad news for the zemmiphobe.

Zeusophobia

MEANING: fear of god

ORIGIN: the Greek god Zeus, king of the gods

ZEUSOPHOBIA is the fear of god, usually caused by a negative experience with god or religion. Forced prayer, threats of divine retribution or the "wrath of God," or anxiety over God's omnipotence can instill extreme fear, resulting in chest pain, hyperventilation, insomnia, overactive bowels, and inability to speak coherently. Zeusophobes tend to ignore the positive in favor of anticipating disaster and worrying about what will happen at the hand of God. The typical zeusophobe avoids churches, Bibles, crosses, and religious artifacts. Zeusophobia is a cross-cultural condition that affects people from all religions around the world. Hypnotherapy and talk therapy have had some success in treating this condition. Extreme zeusophobes are not advised to pray for help.

THINGS TO AVOID: churches; the Bible; Sunday morning television; the Bible Belt; crosses; nativity plays; Easter and Christmas.

|||| Phobia Trivia ||||

Similar to zeusophobia is theophobia, the fear of religions or gods.

Zeus was the king of the gods in Greek mythology and had numerous conflicts with humans, most notably when he decided to wipe out mankind and, with the help of his brother Poseidon, flood the world.

Index of Phobias

Alcohol, 159–61
Alone, 162–63
Amnesia, 12–13
Amphibians, 32–34
Amputees, 20–21
Ants, 164–66

Bad breath, 108–109
Bald people, 186–87
Balloons, 103–104
Beards, 197–98
Beer glass, empty, 40–41
Being contagious, 228–29
Belly buttons, 176–77
Blushing, 84–85
Bridges, 100–101
Bulls, 230–31
Buried alive, 227–28
Butterflies, 142–43
Buttocks, 200–201
Buttons, 135–36

Cats, 7–9
Cell phones, 170–72
Change, 158–59
Cheese, 236–237
Chickens, 9–11
Chocolate, 255–56
Chopsticks, 50–51
Clocks, 47–49
Clothing, 246–47
Clouds, 168–69
Clowns, 53–55
Cockroaches, 130–31
Cold, 92–94
Color white, 143–44
Computers, 149–50
Constipation, 52–53
Contagious, being, 228–29
Contrariety, 259
Conversation, at dinner, 60–61
Cooking, 154–55
Cotton balls, 217–18

Crossing the street, 72–73
Crowds, 79–81

Dancing, 44–45
Darkness, 172–73
Dinner conversation, 60–61
Doctors, 119–20
Dolls, 184–86
Doors, 81–82
Dryness, 254–55

Empty beer glass, 40–41
Erect penis, 122–23
Erection, losing, 155–56
Everything, 181–82
Eyes, opening, 178–79

Failure, 25–26
Falling in love, 192–93
Farting, 91–92
Feathers, tickled by, 198–200
Feeling pleasure, 110–11
Female genitals, 88–89
Fish, 120–21
Flowers, 15–16
Flutes, 27–28
Food, 49–50
Foreign languages, 253–54
Freedom, 76–77
The French, 96–97

Genitals, female, 88–89
Getting rid of things, 70–71
Getting wrinkles, 207–208
Ghosts, 188–90
God, 264–65
Good news, 87–88
Gravity, 31–32
Great mole rat, 262–63

Hair, 41–43
Haircuts, 232–33
Hands, 43–44

Art Credits

All images from Shutterstock.com

page 3, chicken, FoxyImage
page 4, soap, George J
page 7, cat, Croisy
page 15, flower, Morphart Creation
page 23, spider, Channarong Pherngjanda
page 27, flute, Morphart Creation
page 30, slime, Robles Designery
page 32, frog, Morphart Creation
page 36, clown, RetroClipArt
page 42, hair, Morphart Creation
page 43, hand, JRMurray, 76
page 46, money, Alexander_P
page 49, cornucopia, Christos Georghiou
page 52, toilet, Hein Nouwens
page 55, pumpkin, NataLima
page 58, school, Morphart Creation
page 60, dinner table, Morphart Creation
page 63, tree, Morphart Creation
page 66, justice statue, Barashkova Natalia
page 69, undressing, Morphart Creation
page 74, man in jail, Morphart Creation
page 81, doors, Babich Alexander
page 90, woman in parka, zhekakopylov
page 91, holding nose, Danomyte
page 95, balloons, Alexander_P
page 96, Frenchman, Canicula
page 102, old man, jumpingsack
page 107, finger, StocKNick
page 112, sun moon, Channarong Pherngjanda
page 116, travel, Bodor Tivadar
page 118, doctors, Morphart Creation
page 120, fish, ziiinvn
page 124, rabbi, Vector Tradition
page 127, zombie, Cimmerian
page 135, buttons, Marzufello
page 140, string, Bodor Tivadar

page 142, butterfly, Morphart Creation
page 150, otter, Morphart Creation
page 152, music, Morphart Creation
page 154, cooking, chempina
page 159, alcohol, Artur Balytskyi
page 163, mushrooms, Morphart Creation
page 167, clouds, Danussa
page 174, statue, Hein Nouwens
page 180, beard, Stocksnapper
page 183, paper, owatta
page 188, ghost, Iamnee
page 192, couple, Hein Nouwens
page 198, feather hand, Maisei Raman
page 200, buttocks, Hein Nouwens
page 202, hand, MoreVector
page 205, woman and mirror, Morphart Creation
page 206, rabbit, Bodor Tivadar
page 209, hand, Croisy
page 210, vampire, KUCO
page 214, moon, Channarong Pherngjanda
page 221, tunnel, Morphart Creation
page 226, number, Alhovik
page 230, bull, Barashkova Natalia
page 231, shipwreck, Morphart Creation
page 236, cheese, Epine
page 240, urinal, Frolova Polina
page 241, heaven, Morphart Creation
page 244, naked soldiers, Morphart Creation
page 248, witch, Morphart Creation
page 251, banana, vector_ann
page 258, argument, Morphart Creation
page 260, mole rat, Morphart Creation
page 264, Zeus, Betacam-SP

About the Author

Andrew Thompson divides his time between Australia and England. A lawyer by trade, his obsession with finding out the truth about aspects of the world that we take for granted has led him to accumulate a vast body of knowledge, which he has now distilled into book form.

See all of Andrew's books at www.andrewthompsonwriter .co.uk or at Twitter @AndrewTWriter.